At Issue

Presentism: Reexamining Historical Figures Through Today's Lens

Other Books in the At Issue Series

At Issue

Presentism: Reexamining Historical Figures Through Today's Lens

Sabine Cherenfant, Book Editor

GREENHAVEN
PUBLISHING

Published in 2019 by Greenhaven Publishing, LLC
353 3rd Avenue, Suite 255, New York, NY 10010

Articles in Greenhaven Publishing anthologies are often edited for length to meet page
requirements. In addition, original titles of these works are changed to clearly present
the main thesis and to explicitly indicate the author's opinion. Every effort is made to
ensure that Greenhaven Publishing accurately reflects the original intent of the authors.
Every effort has been made to trace the owners of the copyrighted material.

Cover image: gigibees/Shutterstock.com

Library of Congress Cataloging-in-Publication Data

Names: Cherenfant, Sabine, editor of compilation.
Title: Presentism: reexamining historical figures through today's lens /
  Sabine Cherenfant, book editor.
Other titles: Reexamining historical figures through today's lens
Description: First edition. | New York: Greenhaven Publishing [2019] |
  Series: At issue | Includes bibliographical references and index. |
  Audience: Grades 9–12.
Identifiers: LCCN 2018028704| ISBN 9781534503816 (library bound) | ISBN
  9781534504493 (pbk.)
Subjects: LCSH: History—Study and teaching—Juvenile literature. |
  Education—Biographical methods—Juvenile literature. | History—Moral and
  ethical aspects—Juvenile literature. | Historiography—Juvenile
  literature. | Multicultural education—Juvenile literature. | Presentism
  (Philosophy)—Juvenile literature.
Classification: LCC D16.2 .P714 2018 | DDC 901—dc23
LC record available at https://lccn.loc.gov/2018028704

Manufactured in the United States of America

Website: http://greenhavenpublishing.com

Contents

Introduction

Each year, decade, or century brings a new way of life that determines what society prioritizes as its moral standards. Likewise, what is upheld as moral and immoral affects how the past is viewed from the vantage of the present. This practice is known as presentism. It refers to one's tendency to analyze the past with current-day attitudes instead of viewing history from an objective perspective. As explained by Jamin Asay and Sam Baron, presentism focuses only on the present, with a blind eye toward everything that came before: "According to presentism, all and only present entities exist."[1] Therefore, beyond morality, presentism makes us selective about what should be considered true about the past and what shouldn't, which is why many oppose presentism.

Ultimately, the question "what is morality?" is what we are trying to answer when we look at the past and determine where the future will lead us. "How could we ever say, as a matter of scientific fact, that one way of life is better, or more moral, than another? Whose definition of 'better' or 'moral' would we use?"[2] Sam Harris asks at the very start of his book *The Moral Landscape: How Science Can Determine Human Values*. Besides, as Lynn Hunt writes in her argument against presentism, the world as it is today is only a fraction of life. Just as humans alive now in the twenty-first century do not view themselves as a segment of an ever-changing society, those in the past did not either.[3]

Therefore, the question remains: as we look at the past, should we make moral judgments? Should we just accept the past for what it was? This idea, however, clashes with different identities. If ˑ are nonwhite or non-gender conforming, it can be hard ᵗ at the past with no regard for your identity. Where do v all of these historical narratives? Most books on hiˑ written by minorities or women. As society woˑ

down barriers in the present, more voices are starting to be heard, and as a result our understanding of history is changing.

Ultimately, your identity affects your understanding of history and contemporary debates. Though sexism, racism, and homophobia are not confined to the present, they are at the forefront of debates in the twenty-first century. They are issues that affect the bulk of humanity and demand discussion. It can be hard to evoke historical figures without assessing how their past actions reflected these issues that are of great concern today and perhaps influenced the direction these debates would take into the present.

For instance, George Washington is celebrated for being one of the Founding Fathers of the United States, but he was also a slave owner. What does that mean to Americans who are descendants of slaves? Do they have the right to question or disregard his legacy? Do they not have the right? Would the United States be what it is today without the contributions of Washington as president and Revolutionary War hero? All things considered, should we celebrate past historical figures despite their shortcomings? Understanding how past ways of life intersect with people's identities in the present is a key argument for the usefulness of presentism.

However, the primary controversy with presentism is that it jeopardizes the past and the future to prioritize the present. According to David Ingram, "If only present things exist, we can't express singular propositions about the past, since the obvious propositional constituents don't exist, nor can we account for temporal passage, or the openness of the future."[4]

Other questions surrounding this subject include: When it comes to criticizing historical figures, are we simply removing the legacy of some to make space for others, and is it right to do this? When discussing the lack of female representation in history, are we sacrificing male historical figures to compensate? How did the patriarchal nature of the past affect who we celebrate today as historical figures? What do the historical figures we celebrate generally look like when we take factors like race, gender, country of origin, and sexual orientation into consideration?

Those questions highlight why revisiting historical figures could be useful, even if it is merely to create a better understanding of our present sociocultural context. Furthermore, it is worth exploring how certain biases and voids in our educational system prevented us from learning about important historical figures from other parts of the world, as well as how we go about establishing new narratives or finding new historical figures to celebrate. While the viewpoints in this book examine a number of perspectives on the issue, in particular they will examine three subjects where presentism comes into play. They will explore its role in our reassessment of the past through looking at how presentism relates to women's history, Native American history, and the African American experience.

There are many relatively well-known female trailblazers in the world, including Rachel Louise Carson and Rosalind Franklin, but the list of women we get to celebrate as historical figures is scrutinized for its lack of diversity. Intersectionality—the interconnected nature of categorizations like gender, sexuality, class, and race—wasn't a factor taken into consideration in the early days of the women's liberation fight. When examining the suffrage movement through today's lens, questions like how the rights of nonheterosexual women and nonwhite women fit into the fight arise. But what do we gain by questioning the work of past female trailblazers?

Does reexamining the history of feminism mean that we should dismiss those we celebrate as pioneers of the women's rights movement? Even though it is difficult to separate today's understanding of what is right and what is wrong from our understanding of history, are we sacrificing the efforts made in the past in order to make them align with what is considered r¹ today? Also, as we work to improve the representation of v as historical figures, are we overcompensating in the pr giving women an undue role in history? By analy⁷ viewpoints, readers will get a chance to see both si on the female historical figures we celebrate.

Secondly, this volume includes viewpoints offering different arguments about Christopher Columbus and the history of Native Americans. Columbus has long been celebrated as the Italian explorer who discovered the Americas, but were the Americas even discovered, considering that an indigenous population already called it home? This is a narrative that is being scrutinized today. In 2016,[5] more than two hundred Native American groups joined forces to fight the United States' decision to build a pipeline near the Standing Rock Sioux reservation.[6] This event reinforced questions that are being raised today regarding Native Americans' place in the United States' history and present.

Moreover, as Ellen McGirt mentioned in the newsletter *Fortune RaceAhead*, many are ditching Columbus Day and renaming it Indigenous People's Day instead. But this new decision is creating friction in the Italian American community. As McGirt observes, "Many Italian American groups see the holiday as a way to celebrate their own survival as immigrants."[7] Therefore, the issue of presentism raises the question: are we sacrificing the struggle of one group to alleviate the pain of another? Should Christopher Columbus still be credited for the unprecedented voyage he undertook?

Lastly, how does presentism change our view of past historical figures as they relate to race? Even when looking at leaders of the civil rights movement, it is worth examining whether our perspective has remained consistent toward them across history. For instance, Malcolm X was a controversial figure of the civil rights movement. Can we still say the same of him now in the wake of social fights like Black Lives Matter and the rise of racial tension? Has he been made a more innocuous figure in historical narratives, or have today's social movements accepted his confrontational style more than his contemporaries did? Is it possible we would have reacted to him in the same way if he were a public figure in the present as opposed to the past? Looking at a figure like Malcolm X has the potential to help us better discern the role and nature of today's disruptive public agents and activists.

As presentism shifts our understanding of the past, we must ask whether there are benefits to viewing the past through today's lens and making moral judgments. Readers of *At Issue: Presentism* will gain a better understanding of how presentism is defined and the various perspectives on its place in the study of history and contemporary society. Through subjects that are at the center of presentism, readers will find different ways to view the issue and therefore will be able to craft a more informed conclusion on this controversial topic.

Notes

1. Jamin Asay and Sam Baron, "The Hard Road to Presentism," *Pacific Philosophical Quarterly* 95, no. 3 (2014): 314–335.

2. Sam Harris, *The Moral Landscape: How Science Can Determine Human Values*. New York: Free Press, 2010.

3. Lynn Hunt, "Against Presentism," *Perspectives on History*, May 2002. https://www .historians.org/publications-and-directories/perspectives-on-history/may-2002/against -presentism.

4. David Ingram, "The Virtues of Thisness Presentism," *Philosophical Studies* 173, no. 11 (2016): 2867.

5. Justin Worland, "What to Know About the Dakota Access Pipeline Protests," *Time*, October 2016. http://time.com/4548566/dakota-access-pipeline-standing-rock-sioux/.

6. BBC, "Dakota Pipeline: What's Behind the Controversy?," February 7, 2017. http://www .bbc.com/news/world-us-canada-37863955.

7. Ellen McGirt, "The Growth of Indigenous People's Day," *Fortune RaceAhead*, October 10, 2017. https://view.email.fortune.com/?qs=99378e83777bd21e4d227777 d7eab51f07a5af0c01d123d11d8a63faab 2817c79d49f1f3f5ca39524e4c9e87330cd 557c6eb5de5ba096b8818ae424d76bd0819.

1

The Problem with Presentism Is That It Blurs Our Understanding of the Past

Lynn Hunt

Lynn Hunt is a distinguished research professor at the University of California–Los Angeles (UCLA). As part of her extensive research, she has published books on French history and the history of human rights. Some of her most recent works are Inventing Human Rights *and* Writing History in the Global Era.

The primary issue with presentism is that it gives us a biased view of the past and prevents us from having a comprehensive and unprejudiced understanding of people who lived differently than us. By making moral judgments on past historical figures, we are accomplishing a temporary sense of superiority at best while missing the key point of studying historical figures. It is true that since history is unfolding, we gain a better understanding of past events than those who lived during a previous era, but so will those who will live centuries after us.

Who isn't, you say? Hardly any "ism" these days has much of a scholarly following. Yet presentism besets us in two different ways: (1) the tendency to interpret the past in presentist terms; and (2) the shift of general historical interest toward the contemporary period and away from the more distant past.

Lynn Hunt, "Against Presentism," Perspectives, May 2002, American Historical Association, https://www.historians.org/publications-and-directories/perspectives-on-history/may-2002/against-presentism.

Although the first propensity was implicit in Western historical writing from its beginnings, it took a more problematic turn when the notion of "the modern" began to take root in the 17th century. Over time, modernity became the standard of judgment against which most of the past, even the Western past, could be found wanting. The second trend, the shift of interest toward the contemporary period, clearly has a connection to the invention of modernity, but it did not follow as much in lockstep as might be expected. As late as the end of the 19th century, and in some places even after that, students in history expected to study mainly ancient history and to find therein exemplars for politics in the present. Ten or fifteen years ago, survey courses routinely stopped at World War II. French historians still refer to history in the 16th–18th centuries as *histoire moderne*; for them "contemporary history" began in 1789, and until recently, it stopped about the time of World War I, the rest of the 20th century being consigned to the province of journalism rather than historical scholarship. I believe that the 20th century should be part of historical scholarship and teaching, of course, but it should not crowd out everything else.

There is a certain irony in the presentism of our current historical understanding: it threatens to put us out of business as historians. If the undergraduates flock to 20th-century courses and even PhD students take degrees mostly in 20th-century topics, then history risks turning into a kind of general social studies subject (as it is in K–12). It becomes the short-term history of various kinds of identity politics defined by present concerns and might therefore be better approached via sociology, political science, or ethnic studies. I'm not arguing that identity politics have no place in historical study; women's history, African American history, Latino history, gay and lesbian history, and the like have all made fundamentally important contributions to our understanding of history. It is hard to imagine American history in this country without some element of national identity in it. And present-day concerns have helped revivify topics, such as imperialism, that needed reconsideration. But history should not just be the study of sameness, based on the search for our individual or collective roots of identity. It should also be about difference. World history, for example, should be significant not only because so many Americans have come from places other than European countries but also because as participants in the world we need to understand people who are hardly like us at all.

This curiosity about difference should apply to the past in general. The "Middle Ages" or "Ancient World" (themselves presentist designations when they appeared) are not just stepping stones to the "modern" present we know. As historians of those periods know all too well, we must constantly remind students that the Greeks and Romans did not think of themselves as "ancient" and 12th-century people did not imagine themselves to be living in an in-between period of time (except perhaps in relationship to the Second Coming of Christ in Christian Europe). Some of the interest of these "early" periods—but only some—comes from the ways in which people then thought and acted like us now. Much of it comes from the ways in which they differed from us, indeed, lived in ways that are almost unimaginable to us.

Presentism, at its worst, encourages a kind of moral complacency and self-congratulation. Interpreting the past in terms of present concerns usually leads us to find ourselves morally superior; the Greeks had slavery, even David Hume was a racist, and European women endorsed imperial ventures. Our forbears constantly fail to measure up to our present-day standards. This is not to say that any of these findings are irrelevant or that we should endorse an entirely relativist point of view. It is to say that we must question the stance of temporal superiority that is implicit in the Western (and now probably worldwide) historical discipline. In some ways, now that we have become very sensitive about Western interpretations of the non-Western past, this temporal feeling of superiority applies more to the Western past than it does to the non-Western one. We more easily accept the existence and tolerate the moral ambiguities of eunuchs and harems, for example, than of witches. Because they found a place in a non-

Western society, eunuchs and harems seem strange to us but they do not reflect badly on our own past. Witches, in contrast, seem to challenge the very basis of modern historical understanding and have therefore provoked immense controversy as well as many fine historical studies.

Students readily absorb these attitudes of temporal superiority, but they also stand in some ways as our best bulwark against it. When I teach Hegel's lectures on the philosophy of history to students in UCLA's history of history class, they at first seize upon his Eurocentric, indeed racist, comments about Africa's place in world history, but they quite readily see that their condescension toward Hegel derives from Hegel's own worldview. Hegel was the great codifier of Western temporal superiority; for Hegel, all truth is revealed through the progression of history, which means that those in the present always have a better shot at grasping truth than do people in the past. Students understand quite quickly that those who follow them will have the same retrospective advantage over them that they enjoy vis à vis Hegel. Moreover, despite the great upsurge of interest in 20th-century and even post–World War II topics, students still take courses in ancient and medieval history. Whether motivated by escapism, nostalgia, a wish to study "elite" subjects, or just a desire for something "different," they readily throw themselves into another era. In this, they reflect the interests of the general public, which often resents the scholarly insistence on revealing all the foibles of past men and women. They don't always want history to teach them the inadequacies of people in the past or even to reassure them about their own identities in the present. It's the difference of the past that renders it a proper subject for epic, romance, or tragedy-genres preferred by many readers and students of history. The "ironic" mode of much professional history writing just leaves them cold.

Presentism admits of no ready solution; it turns out to be very difficult to exit from modernity or our modern Western historical consciousness. But it is possible to remind ourselves of the virtues of maintaining a fruitful tension between present concerns and respect for the past. Both are essential ingredients in good history. The emergence of new concerns in the present invariably reveals aspects of historical experience that have been occluded or forgotten. Respect for the past, with its concomitant humility, curiosity, and even wonder (as Caroline Bynum reminded us in a memorable presidential address), enables us to see beyond our present-day concerns backward and forward at the same time. We are all caught up in the ripples of time, and we have no idea of where they are headed.

2

Why Judging Past Actions Is Wrong

G.E. Moore

G.E. Moore was a prominent English philosopher of the twentieth century who wrote Principia Ethica, *a book that questions the meaning of goodness and ethics through time.*

To look at the past and designate an action that was considered right in its time as wrong in the present is a mistake because the ethics behind an action should not change over time. If the action was deemed right at the time that it happened, then it should always be considered right. According to this viewpoint, we should look at how that past action has affected society, but if that action offered more benefits than harm, it should be considered an ethical choice.

Against the theory, which has been stated in the last two chapters, an enormous variety of different objections may be urged; and I cannot hope to deal with nearly all of them. What I want to do is to choose out those, which seem to me to be the most important, because they are the most apt to be strongly felt, and because they concern extremely general questions of principle. It seems to me that some of these objections are well founded, and that others are not, according as they are directed against different parts of what our theory asserts. And I propose, therefore, to split up the theory into parts, and to consider separately the chief objections which might be urged against these different parts.

"The Objectivity of Moral Judgments," by G. E. Moore, Fair Use Repository, 1912.

And we may begin with an extremely fundamental point. Our theory plainly implied two things. It implied (1) that, if it is true at any one time that a particular voluntary action is right, it must *always* be true of that particular action that it *was* right: or, in other words, that an action cannot change from right to wrong, or from wrong to right; that it cannot possibly be true of the very same action that it is right at one time and wrong at another. And it implied also (2) that the same action cannot possibly *at the same time* be both right and wrong. It plainly implied both these two things because it asserted that a voluntary action can only be right, if it produces a maximum of pleasure, and can only be wrong, if it produces less than a maximum. And obviously, if it is *once* true of any action that it did produce a maximum of pleasure, it must *always* be true of it that it did; and obviously also it cannot be true at one and the same time of one and the same action both that it did produce a maximum of pleasure and also that it produced less than a maximum. Our theory implied, therefore, that any particular action cannot possibly be *both* right and wrong either at the same time or at different times. At any particular time it must be either right or wrong, and, whichever it is at any one time, it will be the same at all times.

It must be carefully noticed, however, that our theory only implies that this is true of any *particular* voluntary action, which we may choose to consider: it does not imply that the same is ever true of a *class* of actions. That is to say, it implies that *if*, at the time when Brutus murdered Cæsar, this action of his was right, then, it must be equally true now, and will always be true, that this particular action of Brutus was right, and it never can have been and never will be true that it was *wrong*. Brutus' action on this particular occasion cannot, it says, have been both right and wrong; and if it was once true that it was right, then it must always be true that it was right; or if it was once true that it was wrong, it must always be true that it was wrong. And similarly with every other absolutely particular action, which actually was done or might have been done by a particular man on a particular occasion. Of every such action, our theory says, it is true that it cannot at any time have been both right and wrong; and also that, whichever of these two predicates it possessed at any one time, it must possess the same at all times. But it does *not* imply that the same is true of any particular *class* of actions—of murder, for instance. It does not assert that if one murder, committed at one time, was wrong, then any other murder, committed at the same time, must also have been wrong; nor that if one murder, committed at one time, is wrong, any other murder committed at any other time must be wrong. On the contrary, though it does not directly imply that this is false, yet it does imply that it is unlikely that any particular *class* of actions will absolutely always be right or absolutely always wrong. For, it holds, as we have seen, that the question whether an action is right or wrong depends upon its effects; and the question what effects an action will produce depends, of course, not only upon the *class* to which it belongs, but also on the particular circumstances in which it is done. While, in one set of circumstances, a particular kind of action may produce good effects, in other circumstances a precisely similar action may produce bad ones. And, since the circumstances are always changing, it is extremely unlikely (though not impossible), that actions of any particular class, such as murder or adultery, should absolutely *always* be right or absolutely *always* wrong. Our theory, therefore, does not imply that, if an action *of a particular class* is right once, every other action *of the same class* must always be right: on the contrary, it follows from its view that this is unlikely to be true. What it does imply, is that if we consider any particular *instance* of any class, that particular *instance* cannot ever be both right and wrong, and if once right, must always be right. And it is extremely important to distinguish clearly between these two different questions, because they are liable to be confused. When we ask whether *the same* action can be both right and wrong we may mean two entirely different things by this question. We may merely mean to ask: Can the same *kind* of action be right at one time and wrong at another, or right and wrong simultaneously?

And to this question our theory would be inclined to answer: It can. Or else be *the same* action, we may mean not merely the same *kind* of action, but some single absolutely particular action, which was or might have been performed by a definite person on a definite occasion. And it is to *this* question that our theory replies: It is absolutely impossible that any one single, absolutely particular solution can ever be both right and wrong, either at the same time or at different times.

Now the question as to whether one and the same action can ever be both right and wrong at the same time, or can ever be right at one time and wrong at another, is, I think, obviously an extremely fundamental one. If we decide it in the affirmative, then a great many of the questions which have been most discussed by ethical writers are at once put out of court. It must, for instance, be idle to discuss what characteristic there is, which universally distinguishes right actions from wrong ones, if this view be true. If one and the same action can be both right and wrong, then obviously there can be *no* such characteristic—there can be no characteristic which *always* belongs to right actions, and *never* to wrong ones: since, if so much as one single action is *both* right and wrong, this action must possess any characteristic (if there is one) which *always* belongs to right actions, and, at the same time, since the action is also wrong, this characteristic cannot be one which *never* belongs to wrong actions. Before, therefore, we enter on any discussions as to what characteristic there is which *always* belongs to right actions and *never* to wrong ones, it is extremely important that we should satisfy ourselves, if we can, that one and the same action cannot be both right and wrong, either at the same time or at different times. For, if this is not the case, then all such discussions must be absolutely futile. I propose, therefore, first of all, to raise the simple issue: Can one and the same action be both right and wrong, either at the same time or at different times? Is the theory stated in the last two chapters in the right, so far as it merely asserts that this cannot be the case?

Now I think that most of those who hold, as this theory does, that one and the same action cannot be both right and wrong, simply assume that this is the case, without trying to prove it. It is, indeed, quite common to find the mere fact that a theory implies the contrary, used as a conclusive argument against that theory. It is argued: Since this thoery implies that one and the same action can be both right and wrong, and since it is evident that this cannot be so, therefore the theory in question must be false. And, for my part, it seems to me that such a method of argument is perfectly justified. It does seem to me to be evident that no voluntary action can be both right and wrong; and I do not see how this can be proved by reference to any principle which is more certain than it is itself. If, therefore, anybody asserts that the contrary is evident to him—that it is evident to him that one and the same action *can* be both right and wrong, I do not see how it can be *proved* that he is wrong. If the question is reduced to these ultimate terms, it must, I think, simply be left to the reader's inspection. Like all ultimate questions, it is incapable of strict proof either way. But most of those who hold that an action can be both right and wrong are, I think, in fact influenced by certain considerations, which do admit of argument. They hold certain views, from which this conclusion follows; and it is only because they hold these views, that they adopt the conclusion. There are, I think, two views, in particular, which are very commonly held and which are specially influential in leading people to adopt it. And it is very important that we should consider these two views carefully, both because they lead to this conclusion and for other reasons.

The first of them is as follows. It may be held, namely, that, whenever we assert that an action or class of actions is right or wrong, we must be merely making an assertion about somebody's *feelings* towards the action or class of actions in question. This is a view which seems to be very commonly held in some form or other; and one chief reason why it is held is, I think, that many people seem to find an extreme difficulty in seeing what else we possibly *can* mean by the words right and wrong, except that some mind or set of minds has some feeling, or some other mental attitude, towards the actions to which we apply these predicates. In some of its forms this view does not lead to the consequence that one and the same action may be both right and wrong; and with these forms we are not concerned just at present. But some of the forms in which it may be held do directly lead to this consequence; and where people do hold that one and the same action may be both right and wrong, it is, I think, very generally because they hold this view in one of these forms. There are several different forms of it which do lead to this consequence, and they are apt, I think, not to be clearly distinguished from one another. People are apt to assume that in our judgments of right and wrong we must be making an assertion about the feelings of *some* man or *some* group of men, without trying definitely to make up their minds as to who the man or group of men can be about whose feelings we are making it. So soon as this question is fairly faced, it becomes plain, I think, that there are serious objections to any possible alternative.

[…]

This second fact is merely the observed fact, which it seems difficult to deny, that, whatever pair of feelings or single feeling we take, cases do occur in which two different men have opposite feelings towards the same action, and in which, while one has a given feeling towards an action, the other has not got it. It might, perhaps, be thought that it is possible to find *some* pair of feelings or *some* single feeling, in the case of which this rule does not hold: that, for instance, no man ever *really* feels moral approval towards an action, towards which another feels moral disapproval. This is a view which people are apt to take, because, where we have a strong feeling of moral disapproval towards an action, we may find it very difficult to believe that any other man *really* has a feeling of moral approval towards the same action, or even that he regards it without some degree of moral disapproval. And there is some excuse for this view in the fact, that when a man says that an action is right, and even though he sincerely believes it to be so, it may nevertheless be the case that he really *feels* towards it some degree of moral disapproval. That is to say, though it is certain that men's *opinions* as to what is right and wrong often differ, it is not certain that their *feelings* always differ when their opinions do. But still, if we look at the extraordinary differences that there have been and are between different races of mankind, and in different stages of society, in respect of the classes of actions which have been regarded as right and wrong, it is, I think, scarcely possible to doubt that, in some societies, actions have been regarded with actual *feelings* of positive moral approval, towards which many of us would feel the strongest disapproval. And if this is so with regard to *classes* of actions, it can hardly fail to be sometimes the case with regard to *particular* actions. We may, for instance, read of a particular action, which excites in us a strong feeling of moral disapproval; and yet it can hardly be doubted that sometimes this very action will have been regarded by some of the men among whom it was done, without any feeling of disapproval whatever, and even with a feeling of positive approval. But, if this be so, then, on the view we are considering, it will absolutely follow that whereas it was true *then*, when it was done, that that action was right, it is true *now* that the very same action was wrong.

3

Viewing History Through the Lens of Ethics Can Help Make Better Citizens

Marshall Tamuka Maposa

Marshall Tamuka Maposa works at the University of KwaZulu-Natal. Some of his published works are "The Challenges Facing Academic Scholarship in Africa" and "Reflections on Applying Critical Discourse Analysis Methodologies in Analysing South African History Textbooks."

The most difficult task of a history teacher is to navigate sensitive subjects from the past. Moreover, because civic education is also one of the responsibilities of a history teacher, helping students make better moral judgments is a key educational goal. As a takeaway, students eventually should be able to distinguish between right and wrong to become better citizens, and in this case, making moral judgments about the past is useful because it helps students learn how to effectively do this.

History is laden with contentious issues and the history teacher has to negotiate how to handle such issues in almost every class. One of the propensities of both history teachers and learners is to make moral judgments over the historical issues that they engage with. Indeed, history is a subject that invariably carries the burden of civic education and nation-building and this can be done through identifying right from wrong. In this article, I present the thoughts of selected novice history teachers (who have been in service for at most 3 years) in relation to making moral judgments about the past in the classroom. The teachers identify the historical themes that they have considered making moral judgments about. They also explain the approaches that they have contemplated in this challenge. I then utilise Wineburg's (2001) framework on moral ambiguity to explain the implications of the teachers' views. I conclude that while South Africa's history is flooded with moral references that make it almost impossible to avoid making judgments, the history teacher needs a usable framework that they can rely on for teaching all contentious issues.

Introduction, Focus, and Rationale

The history classroom can be a hotbed of contentious issues if one considers the argument that virtually all nations have historical topics that are contentious in some way (Low-Beer, 1999). This leaves the history teacher with the unenviable task of guiding the learners to ensure that the goals of the teaching and learning process are achieved, while making sure that they do not lose control of the class. The purpose of school history is not uniform across countries. However, it can be argued that history is a subject that carries the dual burden of civic education and nation-building—depending on the nation that incumbent governments want to build. Civic education and nation-building, amongst other things, entails providing for learners a framework that they can use in identifying right from wrong so as to become responsible citizens. While societies are guided by various ethics and moral codes inspired by religions and cultures, at a national level the values that determine right from wrong are enshrined in the constitution. For example, the preamble of the South African constitution emphasises the aim to "establish a society based on democratic values, social justice and fundamental human rights" (The Constitution of the Republic of South Africa, 1996: 1). The implication of such a statement is that any South African citizen who acts contrary to the promotion of the identified values can be judged to be acting in the wrong. Therefore the constitution plays a crucial role in providing a moral compass for the citizen of the nation state.

The values of the constitution may then be cascaded into the education system through the curriculum documents. Indeed, in South Africa, the contemporary curriculum documents promote values whose roots can be traced to the constitution. The Curriculum and Assessment Policy Statement (CAPS) for Further Education and Training (FET) History is based on knowledge, skills and values that are worth learning. It goes further to state that school history plays a part in promoting democratic citizenship by:

> *... understanding and upholding the values of the South African Constitution; encouraging civic responsibility and responsible leadership ... ; [and] promoting human rights and peace by challenging prejudices involving race, class, gender, ethnicity and xenophobia (Department of Basic Education, 2011: 7).*

Evidently, the role of school history is not limited to just the development of academic knowledge, but it extends to the growth of a responsible citizen who engages with what is right and wrong from the study of history. It is partly for this reason that history teachers and learners voluntarily, and sometimes involuntarily, make moral judgments as they study the past.

It is on this basis that I set out to understand the thoughts of novice History teachers with regards to making moral judgments in history. At a personal level, the findings from this small scale study are important for me to be able to critique my own thoughts on why I am in the field of history education. More importantly, at a professional level, this study was critical for me—as a history educator who trains history teachers—to be exposed to the thoughts of novice teachers who are still negotiating their own teaching based on the training that they have received. According to Gorman (2004) and Oldfield (1981) issues of making moral judgments in history are more difficult for the novices and the expectation is that they are able to grapple with such issues as they mature more in the field. I should also add that South Africa is a post-conflict country that is still navigating new societal values after years of colonialism and Apartheid and therefore, the teachers and learners still have burning issues to deal with (Mouton, Louw & Strydom, 2012).

The debate that gripped South Africa over the removal of the statue of former Cape Colony Governor Cecil John Rhodes is ample evidence of how South African history is riddled with controversies. For example one headline read: "Cecil John Rhodes: As divisive in death as in life" (news24 Online, 2015-06-01). This national debate was dominated by opinions on whether Rhodes was a good or evil person. Using the Rhodes debacle as an example, history learners are often encouraged to learn from the past, but it should be understood that such learning would mean that they have to make moral judgments about the past if they are to learn what/who was good or bad. I therefore set up this study to find out the history topics that the novice teachers concede making moral judgments about; the reasons why they make moral judgments and the approaches they follow in doing so.

Literature Review

The key concept at the focus of this study is moral judgments in history. This literature review will show that some scholars like Gorman (2004) and Gibson (2011) prefer to call them ethics in history while others deal with value judgments in history (Bentley, 2005). The debate on moral judgments is not a new one in history. In fact, it was at the epicentre of debates in history education about a century ago with Mandell Creighton and Lord Acton as the central characters. Herbert Butterfield was to join in and become another key scholar on this issue (Butterfield, 1931). As early as 1951, Child bemoaned the paucity of moral theory and singled it out as the reason for the contention between scholars such as Lord Acton and Herbert Butterfield. Child (1951) uses moral judgments and value judgments as two interchangeable concepts, but clarifies that what makes moral judgments is consideration of the human factor. In other words, it is impracticable to make moral judgments on events and institutions because they are not human. Gibson (2011:1) further endorses the argument that moral judgments should not be confused with moralising by explaining that, "To make ethical or moral judgments about individuals or a society is not the same as reporting one's subjective responses to that morality." Therefore moral judgments are not the immediate statements of praise or blame that one makes as soon as they are exposed to particular phenomena, but are the end product of a process of historical enquiry (Oldfield, 1981). Therefore in this article, I will referring to as moral judgments what literature also refers to as value judgments or ethics judgments.

Various contentions have been identified in the debate on moral judgments in history. One of the key scholars, Lord Acton, led the school of thought that argued that historical characters (especially leaders) and events should be judged on a particular moral evaluation (Zagorin, 1998). Opposing this view was Mandell Creighton, but more so Herbert Butterfield, who argued, amongst other things that historians should not busy themselves with making moral judgments about the past (Vann, 2004). Therefore, while acknowledging the negligible neutrality there is, the debate on moral judgments has been dominated by either advocates or detractors.

One position advanced, comes from advocates for making moral judgments on historical accountability. They contend that the historian should be guided by certain professional morals and therefore should take past people to task for the decisions they made. Vann (2004) categorically states that a history teacher should take a position about the evil nature of historical experiences such as slavery and fascism, otherwise he/she might be interpreted as condoning them.

Some historians argue that it is actually impossible not to make moral judgments (Low-Beer, 1967; Gorman, 2004). Their argument is that all humans have a moral compass within them and they cannot run away from it. In fact, Tsan Tsai (2011:1) claims that "our moral and historical views are interdependent," meaning that the former influences the latter and vice versa. This would mean that it is as futile to avoid moral judgments as it is to avoid bias, regardless of our attempts. It is also argued that the language that we use is laced with evaluative implications, which makes it difficult for us to avoid moral judgments (Oldfield, 1981). Acknowledging making moral judgments therefore strengthens historical understanding because if history is about the past, present and future, then historians should take lessons from the past in order to understand the present and the perceived future.

It is crucial to understand, as Babbage (1964) notes, that the nature of history is at the centre of the debate on making moral judgments. If history is viewed as objective as scholars such as Gorman (2004) imply, then moral judgments can be applied, but if it is subjective, then making moral judgments becomes complicated. On this basis, Butterfield (1931:1), had this to say about Lord Acton, who was a Whig historian:

> It is the natural result of the Whig historian's habits of mind and his attitude to history—though it is not a necessary consequence of his actual method—that he should be interested in the promulgation of moral judgments and should count this as an important part of his office.

Labelling Lord Acton according to political ideology shows how the study of history goes further than mere academic pursuit of knowledge.

The argument against making moral judgments has been based on a number of reasons. To start with is the debate over universalism and/or locality of morals. Universalism refers to moral absolutes while locality implies moral relativism (Bentley, 2005). Moral absolutes are problematic if one considers differences in that moral compasses are not based on one fundamental. Differences in, amongst other things, cultures and religions, may mean different moral compasses. It does not mean though, that people within the same culture or religion will share the same view. For example, both Herbert Butterfield and Lord Acton were Christians—albeit the former was Protestant while the latter was

Catholic—but they were not on the same side (Child, 1951). If he had to make moral judgments, Butterfield separated the historical act from the individual and emphasised that it is the act that has to be condemned and not the individual (Bentley, 2005). This was a key aspect of his debate with Lord Acton, who according to Murphy (1984) went too far with his assumptions and exaggerations.

There are also problems with quantification of what constitutes acceptable good or acceptable evil. For example, is a historical character who is responsible for the death of two people morally acceptable than one who is responsible for the death of millions of people? If one were to apply religion to moral judgments, as was done by Herbert Butterfield (whose moral compass was Protestant Christianity), then one "sinful" act can be equated to many. In other words, everyone in history is a "sinner" and can be judged negatively for some action that they took. This argument is even extended further; that no one has a right to be making moral judgments about another.

Another related issue concerns determinism versus chance in the historical process. To explain, a determinist understanding of the historical process would imply that historical agents are limited in their historical agency because fate or other forces play a part. Similarly, accepting the role of chance in determining history means that some historical events cannot be fully attributed to historical characters (Oldfield, 1981).

Historians also have to consider presentism while making moral judgments about the past. The difference in time entails that it may be anachronistic to apply the morals of the present onto the actions of the past, especially a past during which the present-day morals did not exist. Gorman (2004) argues that whose morality forms the basis of judgement is not the issue; rather it is about admitting that historians have an obligation to use the historical narrative in order to show social responsibility of historical knowledge. Nevertheless, Gaddis (2002) maintains that our present-day values will always be within us and therefore it becomes ahistorical to try and use our values to make judgments about the past. This view is linked to the argument raised by Bentley with reference to Herbert Butterfield, that moral judgments "must itself be seen in relation to time and circumstance" (2005:67). However, the scholars against making moral judgments argue that we will never know enough about any event, which is why even eyewitnesses can come out with conflicting versions of the same event (Clark, 1967). The versions then get even more varied when later-day historians try to interpret historical sources. According to Child (1951), it is most complicated to make judgments on the motives of historical characters because they are difficult to discern.

Historians also have to negotiate teaching without indoctrination if they are to pass moral judgments. History has been a tool for indoctrination over time in the name of good morals and values which is why teachers are regularly warned not to impose their view on their classes (Richards, 2007). Therefore the scholars against making of moral judgments argue that it tampers with historical understanding. According to Vann (2004), the more the moral judgments, the weaker the historical narrative and hence the poorer the historical understanding.

Finally, according to scholars such as Oldfield (1981), Cracraft (2004) and Megill (2004) historians should not get involved in making moral judgments since they have no training in it and, in fact, it is not really their job. Butterfield (1955:79) stresses this point by referring to the making of moral judgments as "the most useless and unproductive of all forms of reflection." This is in spite of Gorman's contention that "Historians and moral philosophers alike are able to make dispassionate moral judgments, but those who feel untrained should be educated in moral understanding" (2004:103).

Literature has shown that the voice of the school of thought against the making of moral judgments is louder than that of the advocates. Still, the debate rages on—more than a century after it started—and history teachers have to find a way to deal with it in their classrooms. Wineburg (2001) gives an example of a history class where the teacher is faced with moral ambiguity and eventually suggests three scenarios which can be used as a framework for teaching about moral judgments. The first scenario entails the teacher owning up to his moral views and speaking to the learners like a fellow human being who has views on what is good or bad. The second scenario entails involving guests to come and speak about controversial issue under discussion so that the teacher's views are not imposed on the learners. The third scenario is when the teacher does not offer any judgment but gives the class readings and a task so that they express their views independent of the teacher's influence. This is the framework I used in trying to understand the approaches that the novice teachers recommend for use in the history classroom.

Methodology

This was a small scale qualitative study whose focus was on revealing and understanding the thoughts of novice teachers who also happen to be enrolled for the Bachelor of Education (B.Ed) Honours degree in History Education. I therefore worked in the interpretivist paradigm with a view to understand the socially constructed reality of the thoughts of participants (De Vos *et al.,* 2005). The methodology that I employed was narrative inquiry since my focus was to gather the thoughts of the participants based on their experiences in the history classroom with relation to what they were learning in their B.Ed Honours programme. The premise on which I worked was that narrative enquiry enables the participants to manifest their thoughts through stories that they tell without my interruption (Trahar, 2009). I refer to my sample as novice teachers since they were all within their first three years of teaching experience. The participants also happened to have been exposed to and discussed issues of moral judgments in history in one of their core modules. They therefore had an idea about some of the key issues on moral judgments. Therefore I practiced convenience sampling and ended up with a sample of eight novice teachers (Denzin & Lincoln, 2008; De Vos *et al.,* 2005).

Employing narrative inquiry to gather data I gave the novice teachers an open ended questionnaire on which they would write their narratives in accordance with the tenets of qualitative research. The point was to avoid interviewing them since the power dynamic between me as an academic and them as students would have interfered with the trustworthiness of the data. The questionnaire expected the participants to firstly reveal if there are themes/topics in history that they would make moral judgments on. If so, they would then have to give reasons as to why they would make moral judgments while teaching such themes. Finally they had to provide an explanation of the approach they recommended for teaching their chosen topic.

I analysed the data through a qualitative content analysis. I already had three questions which the participants answered, namely: Is there a theme/topic that you would make moral judgments on? Why would you make moral judgments on the identified theme/topic? Which approach would you recommend in teaching the identified theme taking into consideration your position on the making of moral judgments? I used the answers to these three questions as guidelines in coming up with the key themes from my analysis. Within each theme I practised open coding of the data to come up with categories that I present below.

Findings

Choice of Themes/Topics

All the participants agreed that they have made moral judgments and will probably keep on doing so when teaching particular topics. The themes/topics that the participants identified were as follows:

- Pseudo-scientific racism (Participant A)
- Nazism and the Holocaust (Participants C, D, E)
- The My Lai Massacre (Vietnam) (Participant B)
- Wars in the Democratic Republic of the Congo (DRC) (Participant F)

There is need to explain a few issues concerning the topics that the participants chose. Pseudo-scientific racism and Nazism and the Holocaust fall under one theme in the South African School History curriculum. The choice of the My Lai Massacre was not surprising as one of the articles that we had worked with in class referred to it. It is worth noting then that the participants decided not to choose an overtly South African contentious issue. Although I did not ask them why they did not choose a South African topic this choice can be understood as avoidance of contentious issues that are directly linked to South Africans such as Apartheid. Still worth noting is the fact that the student who chose the "Wars in the Democratic Republic of the Congo" is actually Congolese.

Reasons for Topic Choices

The participants gave varying reasons informed by personal, religious, legal, collective norms, social responsibility and historical consciousness. One participant can be said to have given personal reasons for her decision on the topic that she would use to teach moral judgments. For example, in reference to the Holocaust, Participant E argued that "although it happened years ago it still cannot be justified; it is acceptable to make moral judgments … as it is not okay to kill regardless of doing it as obeying orders or not." The participant did not state the moral compass for judging the immorality of the Holocaust. She also did not make a moral judgment on Hitler only but all who participated, willingly or otherwise, in the Holocaust.

One of the moral compasses given by the participants is religion. With reference to the My Lai Massacre, Participant B emphasised "questioning the act of violence" and felt that learners can use "their moral compass not only mentally but through beliefs such as 'God.'" Participant A (who chose pseudo-scientific racism) argued for the importance of the "religious perspective" and Participant D (who chose the Holocaust) supported this view by pointing out that "religion can also play a big role when one would not be able to think." Although the three participants did not explicitly declare their religious affiliation, they revealed how they relied on religion in making moral judgments.

A human rights perspective also came out with two participants referring to laws and conventions. For example, Participant A, who had earlier mentioned his religious influences, stated that,

I feel that it is important today to make moral judgments on such inhuman behaviour and human rights violations … It was unlawful to implement sterilisation policies on other human beings; it is against the United Nations charter of human rights.

Still on Nazism, Participant C had this to say: "Hitler trampled on human rights on a large scale and defied conventional and ethical norms of war." Evidently the two participants prefer to refer to legal documents as their moral compasses, including human rights documents that were penned after the said historical event.

Another perspective that emerged from the data was the reference to collective societal norms. This is evident in such a statement: "Hitler is regarded by many people today to be the embodiment of evil" (Participant C). This means that he also bases his moral judgments on what collective society says about historical events or characters. The participant goes further to show that he refers to present-day society and not necessarily the views of the society contemporary to the historical event by claiming that "Hitler's actions during WW2 is *(sic)* regarded as one of the most immoral acts by present day's society." This would mean that teachers and learners take educational standpoints on the basis of what present-day collective society says.

Social responsibility also seemed to be driving some of the participants' decisions to make moral judgments. For instance, both Participants A and B regarded it as their duty to "raise awareness" about racism and violence which they consider immoral. Meanwhile Participant F considered it her responsibility to "address social, economic, and political problems within society." The participants therefore seem to view themselves as more than teachers, but also as activists who partake in building a fairer society.

Two participants demonstrated that they had not forgotten their primary task as History teachers and they were of the view that making moral judgments actually aid historical understanding. According to Participant A, if moral judgments are made, "learners are no longer unconnected from the past and today actions."

Participant C was more explicit claiming that moral judgments help learners understand:

> ... *ethical issues about human nature, blind loyalty and wilful ignorance. All the concepts above are relevant to many conflicts in the world today and also to many South Africans in both apartheid and post-apartheid.*

Approaches to Teaching Moral Judgments

I had asked the participants to state their approaches to teaching the identified topics on the pretext that their approach would show if they allowed the leaners to make judgments for themselves. This was based on Wineburg's (2001) framework of three scenarios which, as explained in the literature review, offers teachers approaches to dealing with the making of moral judgments.

The students suggested various ways of helping learners to make moral judgments. One of the main suggested strategies was the teaching of empathy. Seven of the eight participants felt that teaching empathy is a key to making moral judgments about the past. Participant D further pointed out that the use of games and role play can enhance empathy skills that in turn help develop making moral judgments. Although Participant F did not mention empathy he suggested the employment of a "leaner-centred approach" exemplified by strategies such as group work whereby learners would make their own judgments as groups then report to the rest of the class.

The participants also suggested that there are other key issues that should be taught. For instance, Participant A argues that the History teacher should "make sure they *[learners]* understand the concept of democracy and the UN Charter on human rights." This shows that the participant would encourage learners to make moral judgments about the past on the basis of the present norms. Participant C who also exhibited presentism by referring to the present-day norms, however contradicted himself when he claimed that it is important to highlight "time and context" in order to "compare present and past norms."

Another strategy that was suggested is the use of "parents, peers and other unofficial sources which students can rely on" (Participant C). This reveals the thought that learners need to be guided by others in making moral judgments about the past. Only one of the participants as noted earlier seems to suggest explicit learner-centeredness. The only other similar suggestion came from Participant A who, after suggesting that the learners should learn about democracy and human rights, then suggested that the teacher should "expose learners to different sources so that they can make their own moral judgments."

Discussion

Five key points of discussion can be extrapolated from the findings presented above. The first one is that the participants stress on the importance of making moral judgments about the past since all of them gave a topic that they would make moral judgments on. Even though they did not seem to be making extreme judgments, the participants can still be argued to be falling within Lord Acton's school of thought that moral judgments should be made in studying the past. They all subscribe to Vann's (2004) view that there are some topics on which the teacher has to make a stand. Only one suggested an alternative pedagogy of bringing in guests to class as per Wineburg's (2001) second scenario. They mostly see it as their duty to teach the learners what is good from bad which means that they would take Wineburg's (2001) first scenario where the teacher owns up to their own moral views speaks to the class not just as a teacher but a fellow human being who cannot hide their own moral compass, such as religion. While this frees up the teachers from pretending not to hold a view, the danger is that making moral judgments for the learners may end up being laced with indoctrination based on the teacher's convictions. It was evident that the participants used different moral compasses and not just the national constitutional values as endorsed in the history curriculum.

The second discussion point is that the participants find it easier to make judgments on topics distant from their lives. Only one participant was an exception—a teacher of Congolese origin choosing to make moral judgments on the wars in the DRC. This was a crucial finding in that he was, incidentally, the only participant who suggested the application of Wineburg's (2001) second scenario of bringing in guests to class. Therefore all the participants did not want to apply moral judgments on topics that they personally relate to. The choice of distant topics can be understood to be evidence of the complexity of making moral judgments or teaching controversial issues. The closer to home and more recent the issue is the more personal it becomes, hence the more contentious it is (Low-Beer, 1999). Making moral judgments about a local issue might seem like making moral judgments about yourself as well and so it is easier to choose a distant issue. This distancing can also be understood in the light of the fact that the participants also made moral judgments on both the acts and the people of the past, unlike Butterfield's (1931) suggestion to condemn just the act, if ever one had to. Judging people and not just their actions, may be more difficult if one considers that history learners tend to align themselves with historical populations (for example, some African teachers may find it difficult to condemn some Africans for participating in the slave trade).

Thirdly, the reasons that the participants gave for making moral judgments are more civic and personal than pedagogic. The weak emphasis on historical concepts such as time and context and the stronger focus on civic issues, such as raising awareness and human rights, reflect the teachers to be conducting a civic duty more than a pedagogic one. Therefore there was evidence of the participants' own historical views being interdependent with their moral views (Tsan Tsai, 2011). Failure to link the moral judgments to historical concepts gives evidence that the participants are still struggling to come up with a balance between the two. If one considers Vann's (2004) argument, it can be claimed that since the participants emphasised a lot on moral judgments, they may teach a weak the historical narrative which can lead to poor historical understanding for their learners. This was also the crux of the argument by scholars such as Butterfield (1931), Oldfield (1981), Cracraft (2004) and Megill (2004) that it is not the job of the historian to be focusing on moral judgments lest they neglect what they consider the more important job of the historian—historical understanding. Therefore, the findings of this research reveal a weakness of the first scenario of teachers owning up to their moral views (Wineburg, 2001).

Fourthly, it was evident that the participants are entangled in presentism. An example is the continual reference to the concept of human rights to a time before the Human Rights Charter was passed by the United Nations. Evidently, "time and circumstance" as raised by Bentley (2005) were not made adequate reference to. The findings are evidence of Gaddis' (2002) point of view on how our present-day values will always be within us and we end up using them, knowingly or otherwise. Nevertheless, the participants could justify their thoughts with Gorman's (2004) argument that it is not a major issue on whose morality history is judged as long as there is evidence of social responsibility of historical knowledge. The argument by Gorman (2004) therefore supports the view that the teacher should own up to their moral views in order to help the learners make judgments (Wineburg, 2001).

Finally regarding the teaching approaches, the participants overtly suggest learner-centeredness on one hand while covertly submitting teacher-centeredness on the other. To explain, while they acknowledge the importance of learners making decisions for themselves, they also view themselves as the more knowledgeable partner who can teach and raise awareness about human rights, fairness, violence and other social, political and economic injustices. These approaches are in contradiction since the participants seemed to be imposing their moral judgments on the learners, in spite of their claim that learner-centeredness would be the best approach. What this reflects is that they seem to realise that the contemporary South African education system emphasises learner-centeredness— and this is not surprising since they have only recently completed their teacher training. However, they are embroiled in the tension that they also know that post-apartheid education should contribute to identifying and correcting the wrongs of the past. This tension is therefore also evident in the framework that I used for this research (Wineburg, 2001). In fact, the choice of approach is not a simple one and may be influenced by other factors such as the topic under focus, the capabilities of the teacher and the nature of the learners in question. The teacher's experience may therefore be crucial in helping them to navigate the challenges they face in dealing with moral judgments in the history classroom.

Conclusion

This small-scale study shows that debates on the making of moral judgments in history are as relevant today as they were one hundred years ago. The study set out to find out and understand the thoughts of novice teachers with regards to the making of moral judgments. The results show that the novice teachers are still grappling with this issue—something that is characteristic of their lack of experience. As far back as 1951, Child (1951) lamented the lack of theory on moral judgments in history. I argue that the participants in this study showed that, even today, novice teachers need to learn more on the theory of moral judgments. However, it is important to remember Wineburg's (2001) warning that even in the hands of an exemplary teacher, the issues at the heart of history teaching can easily take a life of their own, defying our best and most valiant attempts to fix their course. Therefore I conclude that there is a need for history teachers to be always aware of the balance between their civic responsibilities and their pedagogic duties. Indeed, moral judgments are difficult to escape, but if they are to be encouraged as a benchmark for historical literacy, teachers need to be aware of the frames of reference that they are using and their consequences.

4

Our Position in the Present Always Affects How We See the Past

Sarah Godsell

Sarah Godsell is a historian and poet based in Johannesburg, South Africa.

In addition to coming to better understand historical events, another goal among history students should be to better understand the conceptual nature of history and their relationship to it. History should not simply be taught as a series of objective facts to be memorized but should be viewed from a critical perspective. Learning how to think critically is one of the key benefits of a proper history education, so students should be taught to interrogate their perspective toward history and their own positionality. While it is unrealistic to view history with complete remove from the present, students can be taught to be more aware of how the present impacts their view of the past.

The question of how people understand "history" is complex. It involves interrogation of both what a concept is and what "history" is. It is beyond the scope of this article to explore the deep philosophical debates about the nature of the concept. For the purposes of this article, we will take the definition:

> *Concepts are the constituents of thoughts. Consequently, they are crucial to such psychological processes as categorization, inference, memory, learning, and decision-making. (Margolis & Laurence 2014:1)*

Thus, the concept of history encompasses how history is thought of, how it is learnt, what is remembered about it and what decisions are made about it.

It is important to interrogate how students who will become teachers understand "history." There is widespread literature on teaching history in South Africa, including the journal *Yesterday and Today* published by The South African Society for History Teaching since 1983. However, not much exploration has been done into how teaching students understand the very concept of history. This is important because how education students understand history frames how history is understood and taught in the school classroom. Examining how history is understood by education students also assists in investigating what points must be stressed when teaching first years. A similar case study was done in regards to heritage and how heritage was understood by teachers within the subject of history, but this did not investigate what those teachers understood "history" was (Moreeng 2014).

In a larger project, beyond the scope of this article, it will be important to merge their understandings with studies of how children learn to understand what constitutes the subject of history in the school classroom. This article grapples with ideas of how pre-service teachers understand history through examining the process of a 6-week first-year history module, "What is history," and working through students' answers to questions such as "What is history to you?," "What is history in relation to the present?" and "Is history important?" The students' engagement is also explored to show how their understandings of history are steeped in ideology. On the basis of the data collected, I argue that history is understood by the students from a moral point of view, as either "good" or "bad." History, for these students, is thus ideologically imbued with a moral function. I furthermore make the argument that unless critical thinking is taught as a fundamental part of history as a subject, teaching history can be counter-productive to students' learning.

I use the term counter-productive with an understanding that teaching history assists students (both in university and in school) in understanding their relationship to the world. It imbues them with the ability to research, analyse and process information. In particular, the subject of History requires the students to learn different ways in which the world is experienced and lived, as explained in the concepts of subjectivity, positionality objectivity and truth.

When taught well, history as a subject should explain that we all experience the world through the lens of who we are and where, and when, we live. This requires academic and analytical literacy. Although students sometimes possess the basic interpersonal skills, these can falsely indicate language and subject proficiency. Students rather need deep comprehension that comes with perspective taking, academic language and analysis skills (Lin, Lawrence & Snow 2015).

Students use their current understandings of the world to understand the past. This became apparent in some mistakes that arose in students' tests.

[...]

History As Map

First-year students entering into the course mostly, unsurprisingly, exhibit a common sense understanding of history. This was evidenced particularly through an understanding of the concepts of bias and truth, which replaces an understanding of positionality, subjectivity and objectivity that require an interrogation of how the subject (student) understands the world.

When students engage the idea of history as content of uncontested fact, this limits critical engagement with sources and types of knowledge (Bain 2006). This is particularly problematic when ideological positions are disguised as "factual" history, and both taught and thought uncritically. A crude example of this is a high school student who was taught that under capitalism, there are free elections and freedom of religion, while under communism, there are no elections and there is no freedom of religion (M. Msimang 2016, pers. comm., 20 July 2016).

The critical thinking skills that are developed through learning history do not require a post-modern ability to divorce any idea of truth—rather they require a neo-Vygotskyian (Henning 2012) understanding that everything is mediated by signs and symbols, and different factors get in between the subject and the object that is acted upon. In this case, many students seem to understand history as a subject in itself—rather than an object created by subjects. Thus, how students learn what history is can mediate their understanding of their world. The idea that history is logically linear follows from the view that there is one history that is absolutely true and goes one step further towards entrenching the ideology contained in the "History." This leads to the implication that the ideological climate we are living in is the only logical and true way to live. Apart from the fact that this in itself can be dangerous, this flattens what students can learn from history as a subject both in university and in school.

The importance of teaching history lies in the potential to teach students different ways to "orientate" (Ahmed 2006) themselves in the world, to teach history as map, rather than history as fact. This places pressure on the history teacher to find the right balance between content and theoretical engagement with material to equip the students with the thinking skills to research and engage with historical content.

Ideological bias as presented in history manifests in presenting who is "good" and who is "bad." It can be as extreme a cliché as the case of the victor writing history, or how South African history was portrayed under apartheid (Godsell 2015).

[…]

"What Is History?": Questions and Answers

The first-year students in the group sampled for this article appeared to engage a moral understanding of history rather than one that more systematically engages critical thinking skills about the historical texts or information sources. The areas where critical thinking skills have been incorporated into their understanding of history generally involved strong ideas of "truth" and "fact" that are entangled with ideological bias. The process of making meaning of history was most effective when it began with minute processes of the self: history in me, history in my home, the history I am making, the history I will make. Donovan and Bransford (2005) write:

> *Students come to the classroom with preconceptions about how the world works. If their initial understanding is not engaged, they may fail to grasp the new concepts and information, or they may learn them for purposes of a test but revert to their preconceptions outside the classroom.*

There are various ways of creating proximity to history for the student. This will be further explored in another article. This article explores different cues that students have picked up as personally significant, in the classroom, and in their everyday lives, as either positive or negative "aspects" of history, or as entry points into a history that are important to them. This informs what these students think history is. These cues are important because they offer an understanding into how these teaching students relate to history and how they learn historical concepts. They combine an idea of self, a perception of the past and a lens of the present that is generally not interrogated. Importantly, many of these students had not done History as a subject in high school, so their sense of history had been absorbed through everyday interactions with their worlds. The sense of ideology with which history was imbued comes from a societal construction (and perhaps from primary or early high school curriculum) rather than one strictly taught in school.

The presentation of history as static, or unchanging, has been challenged again and again. There is also broad literature on power dynamics in the production of history, and how the way the past is presented often reflects more about the present knowledge paradigms than about the past.

Presentism, History, and Ideology

"History is more about the present than it is of a past. Is it mostly about what we see from the past and it is repeating itself over and over again timelessly." (Student of SOSINA 1 A 2016)

"Presentism" Lynn Hunt (2002) writes:

besets us in two different ways: (1) the tendency to interpret the past in presentist terms; and (2) the shift of general historical interest toward the contemporary period and away from the more distant past.

Presentism is seeing the past through the lens of the present, without taking into account the way that view might influence that history.

As the student points out above, history is always more about the present than it is about the past. The way we understand history is necessarily filtered through the lens of who we are, where we live, how we live and, importantly, when we live. Thus, in South Africa, our struggle and apartheid past are important in our history, as they are still so close in our present. Beyond this, we live in a democratic society, where free elections are held and valued, where we have a progressive constitution and the wounds of systemic, structural racism are open and bleeding.

The current ideology we live in permeates how we see the past and what gets defined as "good" or "bad." I use the above example to explain what I mean by the ideology that permeates how history is learnt. This is an example. This is true of all places and all times. History also only contains what is "thinkable" in a society at a time. This combines with the students' current understanding of what history is.

As the student points out, history is more about the present than it is of "a past." This alludes to the multiple pasts that are flattened and straightened in any one history. The present is the thing that makes one past more relevant than another one. However, through the data in the test answers, it became clear that the present is a very powerful lens through which the students perceive and understand history.

A student's idea of self also has a significant impact on understandings of history. The students often wrote about roots, rootlessness and needing to know where you come from. A significant number of students located history in their own lives by pointing out that they are making history in their families as they are the first people in their family to finish school and/or to attend university. This both roots history in the present and extends it into the future. This opens the question of where, exactly, history is located in these students' learning. This will be dealt with below.

Presentism is what history is supposed to be able to best guard against; however, it impacts most how we experience and mediate our understandings of history. For first-year students, the immediacy of the new university environment, with its expectations and challenges, could heighten the sense of the importance of the present. At the same time, this increases the sense of the importance of history: "History is all the factors in relation with time that make up the current present" (Student of SOSINA 1 A 2016). Donovan and Bransford (2005) point out that:

> Students bring to school tacit ideas of what history is, and that we must address these ideas if we are to help them make progress in understanding what teachers and historians say about the past. (p. 32)

Concepts such as "citizenship," "good citizenship," "freedom," "democracy," "progress" and "hard work" are given in the data as reasons why history is important. These are ideologically rooted concepts, important in our present day society. The ideology of the present time needs to be examined if history is to be taught in a way which ideology can be recognised, if not untangled.

"Good" History and "Bad" History

"The past kills our future." (Student of SOSINA 1 A 2016)

"I feel that if a person does not know his/her history then they are at a terrible loss." (Student of SOSINA 1 A 2016)

The above quotes express aspects of an argument students made in their responses to the question "What is history to you?" This question required self-reflection. The responses were often in the form of an argument the students were framing: history is either a good thing or a bad thing. If it is a good thing, it is something to be proud of, but also generally something unique to "us" (us being either the individual person, or South Africa). If it is good, it has the power to teach, heal and be an example. The moral position of "good" is also ideologically located. It is located in a specific historical narrative. When students write about history as "good," they generally write about how much people sacrificed, or how much we have grown as a country and the need to appreciate that. The "good" is also aimed at making people appreciate the sacrifices and history in a specific way: by being a "good citizen," by working hard, celebrating the history of the anti-apartheid struggle and, importantly, the uncontested victory of that struggle. "Good citizenship" and "good history" requires a celebration of a national history and a compliance with what the nation needs from its citizens: participation in its national narratives.

Interestingly, when students write about history as "bad," it is around the same moral orientation as "good" history. The idea is that the wounds of history are in the past—they have ceased affecting the present, and the only way that they can impact the present is if history is unearthed, discussed in a way that re-ignites pain. In this narrative, the war and the wounds are stronger than the victory:

"But history can also have a bad influence to other people, it can develop hatred between people, for example even today most Blacks hate/blame white people for what happened in the past." (Student of SOSINA 1 A 2016)

The above quote shows another form of presentism that indicates how closely the immediate South African past is tied to the complexities of the present. If hate and blame are so close to the surface, it is surely more to do with the present than with history. The version of the present that offers the possibility for "the good life" requires a specific, linear, triumphant version of history. I argue that Berlant's "cruel optimism" is relevant here.

As Berlant argues, however, the cost of letting go of the idea of "the good life" or as a student phrased it "a bright future," that is attainable *now* is too high. It would involve giving up on a dream of a possible future. Thus, the complexities of the past are relegated to a "history" that can be partitioned off, or "left alone" as it was phrased in class, so it will not impact on the possibilities of the *now*.

This form of presentism undercuts one of the conceptual tools and skills that history necessitates: empathy and understanding that the way we feel and think about the world now is not how people felt out or thought about the world in the past. Donovan and Bransford (2005) write:

> In history we must empathize with ideas we might oppose in the unlikely event we came across exactly the same ideas in the present. If understanding people in the past required shared feelings, history would be impossible. (p. 46)

Here "History" is divorced from the present and only has an effect on the present when people know about it. Also, "History" seems only to exist when and as it is imbued with a moral value. It needs to be imbued with a moral value in order to either be justified or dismissed. When history is assigned a moral value, it judges narratives of events of the past either as either "good" or "bad." However, what emerged from the data was that students took this one step further and judged history itself as either "good" or "bad." History itself then becomes a moral debate and leaves no space for critical thinking and analysis of veracity (Van Eeden 2016). Sometimes these narratives are balanced and combined, but this also still contains the ideological weight and value. One student wrote: "It does not necessarily have to be political to be history or something that holds horrid, solemn memories, but also something to celebrate about" (Student of SOSINA 1 A 2016).

This seems a fairly standard understanding that history contains both "good" and "bad" elements, events and people. However, the evidence in the data suggests that history itself was assigned a moral value by students. It is important—but beyond the scope of this article—to look at what things influence what kind of moral value students assign to history. Moreng (2014) has done this work with regards to heritage.

Where Is the Past? Linear Time and the Proximity of History

> *Students also have ideas about how we know about the past. If they believe, for example, that we can know nothing unless we were there to see it, they will have difficulty seeing how history is possible at all. They will think that because we cannot go back in time and see what happened, historians must just be guessing or, worse, making it up. (Donovan & Bransford 2005:31)*

As a historian, I am particularly bad with dates. I use this in my lessons to stress that history is about more than dates. However, it is important for students of history at all levels to have an understanding of the breadth of history and the sequence of historical events. This shapes an understanding of the concept of causality and how events and actions influence other events and actions. The primary school curriculum in South Africa ensures that students cover histories from a range of different time periods, from the first democratic elections in 1994 to the ancient kingdoms of Egypt, Mali and Mapungubwe. This national curriculum focuses on everyday life in these societies, to present ancient peoples as humans that learners can identify with. This notwithstanding, there is a sense that students in the study have two distinct "locations" for history: one immediate, close, ever-present and so accessible, and one distant and removed, a history that appears to only live in textbooks that teach "world history" with no reference to who the students in the classroom are.

Both these locations arise in the seemingly opposing ideas of disembodied "historians," as well as the potential for everyone to be a historian. The location of history as immediate was expressed again and again in response to the question "who writes history?" While many students labelled people who write history "historians," there was a diversity of opinion over who exactly historians were/are. As we had spent time in class stressing that everyone has their own history, and have their own stories to tell, many students chose the answer "we are all historians." This is helpful in building an idea of the past of the world from the students' own pasts; however, it does locate history very firmly in the immediate past. The sense that history is located in the immediate past is heightened when several students continued their answers by saying "history is written by those who were there." Thus, history is located in people's heads, but then history is a finite thing that moves and fades as people die and memories are lost. This sense of the immediacy and finite nature of history is a problem for teaching students the breadth of the material they will need to be teaching in the curriculum. It also impedes the teaching of critical thinking skills that allow students to apply conceptual tools both to our society today and to Ancient Societies. If history that is seen as interesting and relevant to students only stretches back as far as living memories, the information upon which we construct our world is very limited. It puts great authoritative weight in the narratives of "people who were there" rather than collecting different memories, or different sorts of data, and as well as the need to sort out for themselves what information is reliable and why (Donovan & Bransford 2005):

> *Younger students in particular are likely to assume that history is just known; it is simply information in authoritative books, such as encyclopedias. Forced to consider the question of how we know, they may slip into an infinite regress (bigger and better books) or assume that a witness or participant wrote down what happened on "bits of paper," in diaries, or in letters, or even carved it into the walls of caves. The assumption that the past is given on*

*authority makes any encounter with multiple sources problematic.
If sources are simply correct or incorrect information, all we can
do is accept or reject what is proffered. Sources either get things
right, or they do not. (p. 55)*

So, for these students, history is immediate, following us, tied to
us by what we have lived through and only reliably available from
people who have lived through it. This means that history—our
immediate history, told by people who experienced it—is likely
to be permeated by ideological perspectives. For the students to
discern between ideological perspectives of everyday historians,
and the ideological paradigm of post-1994 South Africa that results
in a sense of "good" history and "bad" history, students need to
understand the historical concept of positionality. This outlines that
each person understands the world through their own lens, which
is constructed out of a complex conglomeration of factors. This is
important in this article, as history, immediate or distant, is taken
as flat and factual. If students do write about positionality, then
they generally write about people consciously distorting history
for their own ends, rather than people's worldview influencing
what history is "seen":

*"Historians can merely be me and the next person. It is usual
that people from the higher places or power structures are the
ones whose decides what to be told or not. People are likely to be
scared to raise their opinions as sometimes these "historians" hides
the truth and only tells or writes what suits them individually."*
(Student of SOSINA 1 A 2016)

The Russian Revolution, the Holocaust, the Vietnam War and
both World Wars are the events that emerged in class when I asked
the students to get into groups to discuss what they considered
"the most important events in history." With the exception of one
group, the events that emerged were events that in the students'
perceptions had limited impact on South Africa, but they saw
as impacting the world as a whole. The events emerge from a
specific historical narrative, one that is also quite close to what
is taught as high-school history syllabus and that is generally

from a European—or broadly Western—perspective. In their written assignments though, when asked "what is history to you?," students wrote about events in their families, in their immediate communities or in South Africa.

Therefore, history, as expressed by the students, is an ideologically imbued immediate sense of the past, where your perception of the present renders the past either "good" or "bad." Alternatively, History is Western-centric and divorced from a sense of who the students are and the immediacy of their lives. Both these locations of history are constrained in the 20th century.

[...]

Conclusion

This article has explored how the students participating in the study view history. It has made the argument that students give history itself both a moral value and the ability to influence events and people either positively or negatively. I have argued that this is detrimental to the critical thinking skills and analysis that history, when taught well, can give students (Donovan & Bransford 2005):

Some students behave as if they believe the past is somehow just there, and it has never really occurred to them to wonder how we know about it. (p. 37)

The group of students in the study locate history as a definitive place, sometimes close, sometimes far, sometimes forgettable and sometimes inescapable. However, with this, the students use history—what is learnt in class and their prior knowledge—to make sense of their own lives. They use the historical content to make meaning of what is happening in the country and what they want or believe they can achieve in their own lives. This indicates that critical thinking skills are associated with the way history is learnt and understood. Ideological climate and learning is also deeply rooted in how history is learnt, taught and understood. Understanding how apartheid systematically and ideologically destroyed lives and livelihoods is crucial for understanding where we are today. The data indicate that the students understand history as either a good or bad thing that has the power to make South Africa a good or bad place in the present and in the future and each individual a better or worse person. I have also argued that this understanding, in fact, contributes to what Berlant defines as "cruel optimism," where the object of desire interferes with the possibility of achieving that desire.

The data also show a focus on individual hard work to achieve a "good life," with history both as a pressure to make use of today's freedom and as a facilitator of today's rights. As history is located in the past—to return to an earlier quote—it can no longer be touched and so the pressure to be good citizens, to work hard and appreciate the good "history" is disguised in the impression of history as a universal and true repository of the past. To return to Berlant the view of the pressure to "fix" and "live up to" the history of the country—as presented through a model of good citizenship—could be detrimental to the ability of an individual to live up to those expectations. In a democratic South Africa, structural oppression and the legacy of colonialism have a serious impact on individuals' abilities to engineer their own lives. In terms of the learning of historical concepts, it is important to be able to divorce ideological trajectories from an idea of what history is. This will allow students to assess their past and present and open up maps for various futures, based on various (factually based, well-analysed) versions of the past.

To have history as an ideological tool is always dangerous. To have history as an unwitting ideological tool—one that is pretending to be inanimate, fixed and scientifically proven—is more dangerous still. And to have this unconsciously as part of how student teachers learn what history is most dangerous. It drastically reduces the potential for history as a school subject to develop critical thinking skills for school learners.

5

Malcolm X's Enduring Legacy

Salim Muwakkil

Salim Muwakkil is an American journalist based in Chicago. Currently, he serves as a senior editor for the Chicago Tribune.

Malcolm X still has a place in public discourse decades after his assassination. However, which aspect of his legacy people latch onto says a lot about how they are positioned in present debates. Through looking at the ways in which Malcolm X has been compared and contrasted to former president Barack Obama, we see that the enduring legacy of historical figures can serve as a point of comparison for present figures and question whether this practice is fair. Furthermore, we see how selecting certain details from a historical figure's biography can be used to make them a tool in present debates, effectively pigeonholing that figure.

Forty-five years after his murder in February 1965, Malcolm X's legacy remains surprisingly vibrant. But that legacy also complicates the relationship blacks have with America's first black president.

There's no doubt the slain Muslim activist would have marveled at the election of Barack Hussein Obama. But there's also little doubt he would be in the front ranks of those protesting the president's race-neutral policies.

Malcolm X (aka Malik al-Shabazz) is most noted for his militant stance in challenging America's racial status quo and his

"45 Years After Assassination, Malcolm X Still a Relevant Figure," by Salim Muwakkil, The Progressive, February 24, 2010. Reprinted by permission.

assertive black pride. Until his assassination on Feb. 21, 1965, he was seen as a kind of counterpoint to the Rev. Martin Luther King's nonviolent activism.

In his first book, *Dreams from My Father: A Story of Race and Inheritance*, Obama spoke well of the slain Muslim activist, although it wasn't Malcolm's ideology that attracted him. "Only Malcolm X's autobiography seemed to offer something different. His repeated acts of self-creation spoke to me," he wrote.

Malcolm's life embodied the message that you cannot become what you need to be by remaining what you are. That message is perhaps the primary reason for his enduring relevance.

His journey from a promising youth in Nebraska to a street criminal in the urban North, to a religion-cursing convict, to a black Muslim convert and evangelist, to an Islamic stalwart seeking global human rights, is an epic one with few parallels.

Malcolm's critique of U.S. imperialism contrasts starkly with Obama's foreign policy agenda, which has amounted to running the system more smoothly than President Bush.

This presents a dilemma for many black intellectuals and activists whose political identities were formed in opposition to U.S. policies seen as racist and imperialist.

On domestic issues, that conflict is compounded. Obama's insistence on race-neutral policies directly defy Malcolm's argument on the need for compensatory policies to redress the historical grievances blacks endured.

Malcolm's portfolio is so varied that various partisans have claimed his legacy.

Black activists cite his influence as a militant alternative to the nonviolent civil rights movement.

Sunni Muslims say he was a major progenitor of Islam in America.

Black nationalists claim him as a leading light.

Contemporary Pan-Africanists list him not far below Kwame Nkrumah as a founding father.

Black studies advocates credit Malcolm for essential inspiration. And leftists note with pride his growing affection for socialism. All of them are right.

And all of them box Obama in.

6

Reexamining Historical Figures Through Social Media

Clarissa Lee

Dr. Clarissa Lee worked as a postdoctoral fellow at Universiti Kebangsaan Malaysia. She specializes in science and technology studies and has had her work published by the University of Virginia Press and Ada: A Journal of Gender, New Media, and Technology.

The innovation of technology and new media like Twitter has helped make the achievements of historical women in the scientific field a focal point. However, it has also brought to light past failures to include women in this field. There are not as many historically recognized female scientists as there are male scientists. Lack of access to education for women is largely to blame, but is it possible that these past issues have created biases in how students view gender and the STEM field? Could reassessing past narratives and historical figures help avoid those biases in the present?

During the Annual History of Science Society 2013 meeting, a round table on social media, "The Pleasures and Dangers of Social Media," was organised as a part of a continuing conversation about the role that social media plays in providing leads for research, in constructing course syllabi, and even for opening conversations about the role of archives in historical research and what that could look like, going forward. Of course, the particular

"Historical Personalities: Tweeting Standard Narratives in the History of Science," by Clarissa Lee, Cambridge University Press. Reprinted by permission.

social media of greatest interest is Twitter, due to its flexibility in public outreach and academic networking.

However, personally, what I find most interesting about Twitter has to do with its capability for the reproduction of archival material, in a manner not unlike the *Wunderkammer*; Twitter can function as placeholders of time capsules where less well-known historical narratives can be foregrounded into other users' immediate consciousness. Unlike Facebook, Twitter is relatively less demanding in terms of its rules and regulations pertaining to who or what is entitled to a personal profile. As one does not have to follow an unlocked public profile to track what they tweet about, celebrities and public figures have taken advantage of this feature to engage in a form of "selfies," whereby memento-mori-like events are captured in their Twitter updates.

Taking advantage of such capability, certain enterprising individuals have decided to make use of the narrative immediacy of Twitter to set up profiles of famous intellectuals and tweet 140-word aphorisms from the latter's corpus of writings. This is particularly the case for historical figures, and the number of them "joining" Twitterverse can only increase with time. Twitter encourages narrative continuity, regardless of the gap between the posts, and is suitable for philosophical musings, existential soliloquies, newsbytes and flash fiction. In fact, the juxtaposition of multiple timelines that interlace and interpenetrate between the layers of your personal tweets can conjure an atmosphere that heightens the punch of the tweet even if it were to be drawn from observations that are centuries old.

One such example is Samuel Pepys, or more precisely, his diary. Whoever is behind the profile has been dropping choice selections from Pepys's diary on the latter's Twitter updates. Ever an artful gossiper, Pepys had a taste for scandal and was not above documenting some of his personal improprieties, bringing archaic, but highly identifiable, humour into the flow of more contemporary tales of scandals and bizarre behaviours. If one is interested enough, one can do a search for history of science personalities with tongue-in-cheek handles (Sir Isaac Newton is known as @MasterofPhysick). However, for others such as Charles Darwin (@cdarwin) and Humphry Davy (@sir humphry davy), the choices of handles are unsurprising.

Some of these profiles are given a more personable aspect in that the individual(s) managing the handles engage in contemporary rapport with other "normal" Twitter users in contemporary dialect, or, in the period-based language of the historical personality. Some of the historical handles are merely conduits for publicising the works of the figure. Some of these figures perform Twitter parodies of "autobiographical" updates on personal achievements and milestones, though unfortunately, their handlers cannot change the automatic manner in which dates are listed on Twitter (Twitter's interface builders either wanted to avoid, or had not considered, historical manipulations).

While one of the more positive use of Twitter has been the highlighting of the lesser known contributions of women in the history of science, through the use of hashtags such as #womeninscience, the focus tends to be more on contemporary women in the STEM fields. In fact, a search reveals that there are not as many historical female figures on Twitter, and this in effect mirrors the standard narratives in the history of science. Of course, there are a number of Twitter handles that take their inspiration from historical female icons, and these handles are usually part of a project or program set up to respond to urgent issues on gender and science. However, it is not as common to find a dedicated handle that is about the life and work of a particular female icon in the history of science. An investigation into these absences becomes more critical given the discussion of the under-representation of women as public intellectuals. Moreover, historically, women's contributions are often submerged under that of their male counterparts because of women's lack of institutional affiliation and access to formal scientific publication. However, women are not only under-represented as a demographic, whether in present time or historically: the whole history of science is presented as a largely masculine affair.

This brings us to the question of why the dominant narratives of history are still the ones to dominate social media: why are we allowing social media to merely amplify social and intellectual preoccupations rather than bring about new ways of thinking? However, this need not be the case, as social media, and Twitter in particular, have the capacity to generate attention towards often-ignored archives that inscribe the voices of the subalterns in the margins: the archives of women and other under-represented people.

Social media can be part of the digital humanities project for performing voices that have been silenced for so long. Histories that were never formally recorded or were buried under the deluge of dominant narratives can now achieve a much-needed visibility. Even as creative writers imagine the multiple ways in which one can put historical figures in conversations with each other, Twitter allows such historical conversations to have urgent immediacy, therefore emphasising how histories are often reiterated merely with changes of circumstance and actors.

Finally, we should ask ourselves what sort of archives of knowledge do we want to build with social media: do we desire to redraw the lines of the history of science or merely echo the products of better-known archives? How can social media be used as a supplementary tool for showcasing research on marginal figures and historical narratives (after all, we can now attach videos, photos and instagrammed visuals to our Twitter updates), and as a form of outreach on the history of science at the margins?

7

Is the Past to Blame for Limiting Whom We Celebrate as Historical Figures?

Ama Biney

Dr. Ama Biney is a professor in the United Kingdom who focuses on African diaspora history. Some of her published works are The Political and Social Thought of Kwame Nkrumah *and* Speaking Truth to Power: Selected Pan-African Postcards of Tajudeen Abdul-Raheem.

In this viewpoint, Dr. Ama Biney offers a comprehensive look at the backstory of Josina Muthemba Machel and discusses how the patriarchal nature of society has allowed female African historical figures to go unnoticed. This viewpoint also highlights another issue close to presentism. Is the problem of underrepresentation the result of the way the past was structured, or is the heart of the problem the way we currently learn about the past? Do our present biases prevent us from learning about important historical figures from other parts of the world, and do we need to address this void in the educational system?

Josina Muthemba Machel was a revolutionary Mozambican fighter for FRELIMO who like thousands of women fought for independence for her country until she died at the tender age of 25. 7 April marks the day she died—a day celebrated as National

"Uncovering Josina Machel from Obscurity," Fahamu Trust's Weekly online newsletter, Pambazuka News, Author Ama Biney, Phd., April 3, 2014. Reprinted by permission.

Women's Day in Mozambique. It occasions a celebration of her exemplary short life.

HIS story (otherwise commonly known as history), continues to tell narratives and accounts of the past from a male perspective. Dismissive accounts may mention African female warriors, priestesses, and queens as footnotes or in passing and then move on to focus on the "great men of history," for ingrained in many is the notion that men make history, and our notion of leaders is unconsciously and unquestioningly male. As we continue to live in a patriarchcal world, the values, attitudes and beliefs that enshrine male thinking, priorities and approaches have become internalised by all—women included. Whilst African women are politically represented in large numbers in a few African parliaments such as in South Africa, Rwanda, Mozambique and Uganda, out of 55 African states, the dismal reality is that there only three female heads of states (in Liberia, Malawi and the Central African Republic). Similarly fields such as architecture, engineering, the sciences, philosophy, political science and history remain male dominated, particularly on the African continent.

The Invisibility of African Women in HIS Story

The role of African women in the myriad nationalist movements, whether the Rassemblement Democratique African (RDA) of the former Francophone countries, or the women's wings of the Convention People's Party (CPP) of Ghana or the Kenya African National Union (KANU) of Kenya—these histories and the women involved in these women's wings, that were often appendages of the nationalist parties, need to be popularly known. The names of women in these movements remain in the background, or wholly unknown, whilst the male names of Kwame Nkrumah, Amilcar Cabral, Frantz Fanon, Jomo Kenyatta, Patrice Lumumba and many others have become household names. It still remains the case that apart from Yaa Asantewaa, the great warrior woman of Ghana, or Queen Nzinga of Angola or Nehanda of Zimbabwe, the names of African women who made history are relatively unknown or do not come readily to mind as those of male heroes. Yet, they are there. Among them is the life and contribution of Josina Abiathar Muthemba who tragically died on 7 April 1971 at the very young age of 25. This year marks 79 years since her birth on 10 August 1945. I stumbled across Josina Abiathar Muthemba whilst surfing the net some three years ago. It made me reflect on why I had not heard about her when I was doing my first degree in African Studies back in the early 1980s, nor when I became active in the London based Black Action for the Liberation of Southern Africa (BALSA). The question: Why isn't she known outside of Mozambique? became a quest to make her known to the rest of Africa and global humanity.

Her inspirational life is perhaps representative of the thousands of female combatants who joined not only the Front for the Liberation of Mozambique (FRELIMO) after it was formed in June 1962, but also the Movimento Popular de Libertacao de Angola (MPLA) of Angola, the Partido Africano da Independencia da Guine e Cabo Verde (PAIGC) of Guinea Bissau, or the Zimbabwe African National Union (ZANU) and the Zimbabwe African Political Union (ZAPU) who should not become forgotten in the annals of Pan-African history. Their names, voices, memories, experiences and deeds have almost been erased and silenced out of patriarchal history. It is only in the last 30 years or so, that is, since the 1980s, academic studies have begun to unearth the lives of African women. However, such studies often remain within ivory towers, for the challenge is to disseminate knowledge and awareness of our history to the greater majority of African people across the African continent and in the Diaspora.

Who Is Josina Abiathar Muthemba?

Josina Abiathar Muthemba was born in Vilanculos, Inhambane, in the southern part of the country, into a family committed to anti-colonial activism. Her grandfather was a Presbyterian lay preacher who like several African clergy across the continent was virulently opposed to colonial rule; her father was a nurse in Gaza province. Unlike the majority of young Mozambican girls she was privileged in being able to go to primary school for 'assimilados' at the age of 7 in Mociboa da Praia, a port town in northern Mozambique. Thereafter she moved to the capital, Lourenco Marques (now Maputo) to live with her grandmother in order to pursue her education. Her family was considered part of the "assimilados" (Portuguese for assimilated) who were granted the honorary status of whiteness by the colonial Portuguese authorities as opposed to being "indigena" or "native." "Assimilados" could include Asians and individuals of dual heritage i.e. one parent being European and the other being African. Eduardo Mondlane describes in his book *The Struggle for Mozambique* the abysmal system of education in Mozambique, pointing out that "although nearly 98 per cent of the population of Mozambique is composed of black Africans, only a small proportion of children attending primary school are African, while the number of Africans in secondary school is almost negligible."[1]

Josina was one of the very few African girls who were fortunate to receive technical secondary education. She remarks: "My parents made a great many sacrifices to send me to school. I went to commercial school for five years. My parents had to save on food and clothes. At the primary school there were only about twenty of us Africans to about a hundred Portuguese. At the commercial school there were about fifty Africans to several hundred Portuguese."[2] An astute student, Josina was fully aware of the objectives of colonialist education. She observed: "The colonialists wanted to deceive us with their teaching; they taught us only the history of Portugal, the geography of Portugal; they wanted to form in us a passive mentality, to make us resigned to their domination. We couldn't react openly, but we were aware of their lie; we knew that what they said was false; that we were Mozambicans and we could never be Portuguese."[3] At the age of 13 whilst at school she became active in the organisation Núcleo dos Estudantes Africanos Secundários de Mocambique (NESAM) that Eduardo Mondlane (later to become the first President of FRELIMO) had helped establish in 1949.[4]

This organisation encouraged, under cover, a positive sense of cultural identity and political education among Mozambican students. It was small in membership and closely monitored by the Portuguese police. As Mondlane remarks, it was crucial in disseminating nationalist sentiments, asserting a national culture, and "provided the only opportunity to study and discuss Mozambique in its own right and not as an appendage of Portugal's."[5] At the age of 18, the politicised Josina fled the country with other students in order to join FRELIMO in Tanzania. Among her comrades were the future President of Mozambique, Armando Guebuza, and seven others (both young men and women). They failed in their endeavours for after a journey of 800 miles they were arrested at Victoria Falls in Northern Rhodesia and returned to the brutal hands of the Portuguese authorities in Lourenco Marques.

A six month stint in prison in which she was not sentenced or condemned[6] was ended by the campaign for her release by FRELIMO that led to her release shortly before her 19th birthday. She was now under surveillance by the Portuguese police. Wholly undeterred, the courageous Josina made another attempt to flee with fellow students. They endured a period of time in refugee camps in Swaziland and Zambia; dodged the Portuguese security police and betrayal by informants. In Botswana the British colonial authorities sought to deport them but again the intervention of the adept FRELIMO leader, Eduardo Mondlane and campaigning by the Organisation of African Unity (OAU) and UN ensured the group of 18 students were allowed to enter Tanzania and then Zambia and finally Dar es Salaam. This tortuous journey of 2000 miles, that is from Mozambique to Tanzania—via several neighbouring countries—is a testament to the will of Josina and her commitment to seeking an end to Portuguese domination of her country.

Working for Liberation

Immediately, the young Josina—at the age of 20—took up post as assistant to the director of the Mozambique Institute in Dar es Salaam. The director, was no other than, Janet Mondlane, the American wife of the leader of FRELIMO. The two became close friends. As Stephanie Urdang writes, it is Josina who "is credited for being the driving force and vision behind the establishment of the Women's Detachment (Destacamento Feminino) in 1967."[7] In the words of Josina: "At first this [i.e. the Women's Detachment] was merely an experiment to discover just what contribution women could make to the revolution—how they would use their initiative, whether they were in fact capable of fulfilling certain tasks. The "experiment" proved highly successful and this first group of women became the founder members of the Women's Detachment and were scattered in throughout the interior, each with her specific assignment. It was soon discovered that they would play a very important role in both the military and political fields but especially the latter."[8] In African societies, women overstepping their traditionally prescribed roles as homemakers and rearers of children, threatened the patriarchal status quo. However, there was also the reality that some men were fearful of joining the national liberation struggle and fighting on the battle field. Josina remarked that: "The presence of emancipated women bearing arms often shames [men] into taking more positive actions."[9]

The Women's Detachment remained small and was more successful in mobilising young women, particularly women without children, than the general population of women. It was opposed by conservative elements within the Central Committee of FRELIMO as the first batch of women, including Josina went to Nachingwea, the name of the military training camp in southern Tanzania for training in 1967.[10] It was in the liberated area of Cabo Delgado in northern Mozambique, where Josina trained that she met Samora Machel. He was director of the training center in the province. With other women combatants Josina not only engaged with the local population in the liberated areas in describing and clarifying the role of FRELIMO, its objectives, its history in order to win hearts and mind to the revolutionary cause, but she and others guarded supplies and organised the community. It is in 1968 that Josina identified the need for organised health centers, schools and child care provision within the liberated zones, to address the needs of the wounded and traumatised victims and soldiers of war as well as the children who had become orphans. In short, a social program commenced which is attributable to the visionary perspicacity of Josina. In July 1968 she was nominated a delegate to the Second FRELIMO Congress held in Niassa province and she made an uncompromising stand for the full participation of women in the struggle for the liberation of Mozambican society and its transformation. As Mondlane observes: "Here for the first time in our history Mozambicans from all over the country were gathered, to discuss together the problems of the whole nation and take decisions which will affect its future. Delegates were from different tribes and the different religious groups, and there were women participating as well as men."[11]

This was a major achievement in the years since the founding of FRELIMO in Tanzania back in 1962. A number of radical resolutions were made at this Congress on the armed struggle; administration of the liberation zones; national reconstruction; social affairs and on foreign policy.[12] Josina was made head of the Women's Section in FRELIMO's Department of International Relations at the age of 24. This post required her to travel outside the country to international gatherings relating to women's rights and she spoke on the experiences and realities of Mozambican women and people from her own first-hand knowledge. She consistently advocated for women's equal participation in political, economic and social life. The year 1969 was an eventful year in her life for in May 1969 she married Samora Machel in southern Tanzania. In November of that year they had a son, named Samito. As Sarah LeFanu writes: "electricity sparked between them" and can be visually seen in photographs of the two.[13] She was also appointed head of FRELIMO's Department of Social Affairs and she continued to develop child care and educational centers for children in the north of the country. She encouraged girls to attend school, which was one of the resolutions passed at the Second Congress. Despite giving birth, the indefatigable Josina resumed work almost immediately in the provinces of Niassa and Cabo Delgado whilst their son was looked after in Dar es Salaam. Meanwhile, her health declined rapidly. LeFanu writes: "It's not clear—versions differ—whether Josina was suffering from liver cancer or from leukaemia. Either would have been fatal." She died in Dar es Salaam on 7 April 1971, aged 25. The impact of her death on her ideological partner, Samora, was profound. In a new film on Samora Machel, Graca Machel (future wife of Samora) describe Josina as "the love of his life."[14]

A year after Josina's death when Oscar Monteiro gave a speech in 1972 at a FRELIMO Central Committee meeting, Monteiro recalled how when Marcelino dos Santos spoke Josina's name in the list of the fallen camaradas, Samora broke down and wept and it was necessary to adjourn the meeting.[15] In honour of Josina's memory, Samora Machel wrote a beautiful poem entitled "Josina, you are not dead." Part of it reads: "Thus more than wife, you were to me sister, friend and comrade-in-arms. How can we mourn a comrade but holding the fallen gun and continuing the combat. My tears will flow from the same source that gave birth to our love, our will and our revolutionary life. Thus these tears are both a token and a vow of combat. The flowers which fall from the tree are to prepare the land for new and more beautiful flowers to bloom in the next season. Your life continues in those who continue the Revolution." If Josina had not married the great Machel she would have remained a revolutionary icon for Mozambican women for her life was remarkable for someone tremendously committed to a revolutionary cause and who died so young when she had a phenomenal capacity to give far more and do much more in building a new society of new moral men and women. To put it differently Josina was a political activist in her own right; with a mind and agency that she determined and put in the service of the betterment of her society.

Continuing Revolution in Myriad Ways

An assiduous reconstruction of African history—that is, what happened in our past and why—needs to rescue from historical obscurity, to remember and document, the women who contributed significantly to the liberation of their societies. Not only do our youth need to know the contributions of those who went before us, but often the adults are equally unknowing and need to be educated. Continental Africans and people of African descent outside of the continent need to immerse themselves in a deep knowledge and awareness of their past that encompasses a Pan-African historical understanding. The great Walter Rodney said: "A people's consciousness is heightened by knowledge of the dignity and determination of their fore parents." For if our fore parents could realise their dreams in struggle—why can't we today? This is the powerful weapon of history that the ruling class seek to keep hidden from ordinary people, for if the masses had a genuine awareness and knowledge of their history it would empower them to begin to change the realities confronting them. One of the tragedies of African people is that enslavement and colonialism disconnected us from history; a sense of where we came from; our own accomplishments; our own ethics, morality, culture and systems in the past. Our psyches and mind-sets have been altered and disfigured by this interaction and intrusion into our history. One of the many challenges for Africans is to know ourselves and our past; heal and repair ourselves from the spiritual and psychological damage and lack of knowing as we reconstruct our continent and its resources to meet the primary needs of the majority of our people rather than outsiders. Among the challenges of Africans is overhauling our colonial mind-set or emancipating ourselves from mental slavery. Perhaps future African film makers and documentary makers in the tradition of Sembene Ousmane will use film as a powerful medium to capture the minds and hearts of African people by portraying the lives of Josina Machel and the other plethora of hidden sheroes and heroes of African history. That would be an inspiring way to continue the revolution Josina took part in. Film makers could educate a new generation of the life and historical context of this important revolutionary figure.

Notes

1. Cited in *The Struggle for Mozambique* by E. Mondlane, Penguin Books, 1969, p. 65.

2. Ibid, p. 66.

3. Ibid, p. 113.

4. Ibid, p. 113.

5. Ibid, p. 114.

6. Ibid, p. 114.

7. See *And Still They Dance: Women, War, and the Struggle for Change in Mozambique,* Earthscan Publications Ltd, 1989, p. 95.

8. Ibid, p. 95.

9. Ibid, p. 96.

10. See *Mozambique: The Revolution Under Fire* by Joseph Hanlon, Zed Books, 1984, p. 31. See also "Nachingwea" in *S Is for Samora: A Lexical Biography of Samora Machel and the Mozambican Dream* by S. LeFanu, Hurst & Co, 2012, pp. 163–167.

11. See *The Struggle for Mozambique* p. 188.

12. Ibid, pp. 189–196.

13. See *S Is for Samora: A Lexical Biography of Samora Machel and the Mozambican Dream* by S. LeFanu, Hurst & Co, 2012, p. 100.

14. See the film *Comrade Presidente* by the Zimbabwean film director, Mosco Kamwendo.

15. See *S Is for Samora* p. 102.

8

Presentism Helps Women Reclaim Recognition for Their Work

Stéphanie Thomson

Stéphanie Thompson is a former staff writer and commissioning editor at the World Economic Forum. She currently works as an editor at Google.

The lack of female historical figures can be explained by the struggle for women to find recognition for their work, but there is also a tendency to be selective about the women we choose to celebrate. Even though the names of women like Shirley Chisholm, Hedy Lamarr, and Huda Shaarawi are not as familiar as those of other female historical figures, they are arguably as important to history as Joan of Arc, Queen Elizabeth I, and Cleopatra. Therefore, one of the benefits of presentism may be its ability to bring to light the achievements of past historical figures that we have neglected.

They say history is written by the victors. Perhaps that's why our history books tend to be dominated by men, with women relegated to bit parts. Of course, there are exceptions: women so powerful and influential that their legacies live on. Queen Elizabeth I, Boudica or Joan of Arc, for example.

Women's rights activist Emmeline Pankhurst is another notable exception. Pankhurst, alongside thousands of women who were part of the suffragette movement, campaigned throughout the

"These Women Changed the World—and You've Probably Never Heard of Them," by Stéphanie Thomson, World Economic Forum, March 6, 2018. Reprinted by permission.

late 19th and early 20th century to win the right for women in the United Kingdom to vote.

On 6 February 2018, Britain marked 100 years since the Representation of the People Act, which gave women over the age of 30 that right. In 1928 women achieved equal voting rights with men.

Beyond these few well-known figures, there are many trailblazing women you've probably never heard of—which is why we celebrate Women's History Month every March and International Women's Day on 8 March.

So who are some of these incredible women you didn't learn about in history class?

Shirley Chisholm

The daughter of immigrants, Shirley Chisholm was born into poverty in Brooklyn, New York City. After graduating with a Bachelor of Arts, she taught in a nursery school while studying for her Master's at Columbia.

She later got into politics, and would become the first African-American woman elected to the US Congress, and the first woman and black person to run for the Democratic Party's presidential nomination.

"I felt that the time had come when a black person or a female person could and should be president of the US—not only white males. I decided somebody had to get it started," she said in an interview years later.

While her bid was unsuccessful, she laid the foundations for those who would come after her, teaching them that anything was possible.

Hedy Lamarr

At the height of her career as a Hollywood actress, Hedy Lamarr was known as "the most beautiful woman in the world." But she was far more than a pretty face. According to her biography, Lamarr was quite the entrepreneur: "She was constantly looking at the world and thinking: Well, how could that be fixed? How could that be improved?"

It was this curiosity that pushed her to try and invent something that would make a positive difference during the Second World War. With her partner at the time, she drew on the mechanics of the piano to create a "frequency-hopping spread-spectrum" system—a device she hoped would protect Allied radio communications from being intercepted by Axis forces.

Although she was granted a patent for the design, the US Navy didn't take the invention seriously. Which was a big mistake—the same technology now underpins both cell phones and Wi-Fi. Years later, she received her long-overdue recognition when she won the Pioneer Award by the Electronic Frontier Foundation.

Sojourner Truth

In 2014, the *Smithsonian* magazine voted her one of the 100 most influential Americans of all time. But outside of the United States, few people will have heard of Sojourner Truth, an African-American abolitionist and women's rights campaigner.

Born into slavery, she was separated from her family when she was nine. Twenty years later, and still living in slavery, she had a vision of Jesus calling her to freedom. She managed to escape and went on to become one of the leading voices in the campaign to end slavery and women's rights.

In 2009 she became the first black woman honoured with a bust at the US Capitol. At the ceremony, Nancy Pelosi explained the statue's importance: "Every person who visits the Capitol of the US will know her important role in America's history, and will see her as an inspiration for the work left undone to fight injustice, hatred and cruelty in our society and in the world."

Huda Shaarawi

Cleopatra might be the most famous Egyptian woman, but her compatriot Huda Shaarawi was just as influential in her time.

As was the norm for upper-middle-class women in Egypt, Shaarawi spent much of her younger years living inside a harem. It was here that her resentment of Egypt's patriarchal society began. She would write in her memoirs years later that "being a female became a barrier between me and the freedom for which I yearned."

Shaarawi was determined to bring down that barrier. In 1908, she founded the first philanthropic organization run by women. Two years later, she opened a school for girls. At the same time, through her husband's work as a politician, she became more involved in the fight against British colonialism. In 1919, she organized the largest women's protest against British rule.

After Egypt won its independence, she went back to focusing on women's issues, setting up the Egypt Feminist Union, the first nationwide feminist movement in the country. One of her most famous acts was to remove her veil—at the time a requirement for women—in front of a crowd in Cairo. Within a decade, few women in Egypt still wore the veil.

Lilian Bland

Don't be fooled by the name: Lilian Bland's life was far from boring. A sports photographer and journalist, she once tried to ride in the Grand National, but was turned away because she was a woman.

Undeterred, she decided to try her hand at something else: flying. She had closely watched the success of Louis Blériot, the first man to fly a plane between continental Europe and the UK, and decided to follow in his footsteps. A year after his record-setting feat, she designed and built her own plane, the ironically named Mayfly.

It may have been made of an empty whiskey bottle and her aunt's ear trumpet, for want of a real petrol tank, but it did the job. Bland became the first women in the world to design, build and fly an aircraft.

9

Historical Narratives Offer a Skewed View of the Past That Presentism Can Fix

David A. Tomar

Tomar is the chief magazine editor of the Quad. *He is a veteran journalist who has covered music and education extensively. His most famous work is* The Shadow Scholar, *which covers the failures of the US educational system.*

Is it possible to overcompensate in representing historical female figures, either by giving them too much credit for the work they did and making them seem more important than they actually were or by ignoring important male historical figures to make room for women? These questions are crucial to understanding the controversies surrounding presentism. But in this viewpoint, Tomar offers instances in which women's contributions to society were overshadowed because of their gender, including the infamous case of Rosalind Franklin. In doing so, he suggests that the benefits of acknowledging the overlooked contributions of historical women outweigh the possible issues.

D id you ever get the sense that your history books are just one big boys club, filled with accomplishments by men, for men, and often to the exclusive benefit of men? Does it sometimes feel like the annals of human experience are simply a fraternity where guys are free to banter about sports and make crude noises without fear of offending the fairer sex?

And if it does feel that way, where are all the women? Did women really do nothing more than pop out babies and make pot roasts from the dawn of civilization until Cher overshadowed Sonny Bono in popularity and the whole world changed?

Of course not. It's just that human history is littered (and I do mean littered) with greedy men who stole their very best ideas from brilliant women.

And in many cases, they didn't just steal these ideas. They published them in journals, won prizes for them, earned millions from them, became noteworthy men of their time, and iconized in retrospect. Meanwhile, the women whose ingenuity, insight, and intelligence they appropriated were more often than not footnoted, both in reality and through the lens of history.

But we wish to correct the record, both because education is all about that unending quest for truth and because a future in which women earn equal credit, respect, and financial compensation begins by acknowledging the sins of our past.

So with that, we spotlight women of stellar accomplishment who should be far more famous and celebrated than they are:

Rosalind Franklin: The Double Helix

One of the most important scientific revelations of the twentieth century has also long been a subject of disputed credit. Famously, Cambridge University scientists James D. Watson and Francis H.C. Crick are credited with uncovering the double helix formation that would catapult forward our understanding of human DNA. In fact though, British chemist and X-ray crystallographer Rosalind Franklin had been engaged in the study of DNA over at Kings's College in London in 1951 when she produced a groundbreaking image. A colleague showed this image to Watson and Crick without permission. This was the turning point in their research, though when they published their earth-shattering findings in 1953, they gave only passing reference to Franklin's contributions. In perpetuity, it is the Cambridge pair that is associated with the double helix. So says the Nobel Prize they received in 1958, four years after Franklin died of ovarian cancer.

Lise Meitner: Nuclear Fission

As long as we're on the subject of scientific genius, there's the story of Lise Meitner. It's hard to say whether Meitner is better or worse off for having been slighted by a greedy man. Meitner was a student under the legendary physicist Max Plank, and the first German woman to hold a professorship at a German University. As the Nazis rose to power, the young Jewish scientist was forced to flee her home country. She continued to correspond with her research partner, Otto Hahn, from her new location in Scandinavia. In 1938, Hahn and Meitner joined forces to outline the concept of nuclear fission. This was the groundbreaking moment that would, in just five years, give rise to the awesome destructive capacity of the atomic bomb. Anybody looking to send angry letters to those responsible would find only Hahn's name on the landmark paper revealing the discovery. Hahn chose to omit his partner's name and was thus the sole recipient of the 1944 prize in chemistry from the Royal Swedish Academy of Sciences.

Hedy Lamarr: Radio Guidance System

Meitner wasn't the only woman working to build military might during World War II. She is joined by Austrian-born, American actress Hedy Lamarr, who in addition to becoming a star of the Silver Screen during the Golden Age of Hollywood, collaborated with composer George Antheil to create a radio guidance system for Allied torpedoes. The Navy pretended it wasn't interested in the technology, but of course it was. They stole Lamarr and Antheil's idea, classified the patent and, by the 1960s, had begun to incorporate the technology into a host of new weapons systems. Perhaps even more importantly, Lamarr and Antheil's work would be nothing less than the basis for the omnipresent Wi-Fi, CDMA, and Bluetooth wireless technologies.

Margaret Knight: Paper Bag Machine

Not all of history's greatest female inventors worked in the military. Margaret Knight made her greatest contributions to production in an era where industry ruled. Often referred to as Lady Edison, Knight was a well-known inventor, mostly because she had the wherewithal to stand up for her rights. In 1868, Knight was working for the Columbia Paper Bag Company when she invented a machine that automatically folded and glued paper bags into the formation familiar to shoppers today. As Knight worked toward the completion of a metal prototype, a machinist named Charles Anan visited her plant. Unbeknownst to Knight, the random machinist filed for a patent for her invention. She only learned of his deception when she applied for her own patent. Fortunately for Knight, many witnesses were on hand as she worked through her invention. This proved more than compelling in a judgment that ultimately awarded the patent—and all future royalties—to Knight.

Elizabeth Magie: Monopoly

In the 1930s, Parker Brothers introduced the game *Monopoly* to American families. The game made a millionaire out of an unemployed heater salesman named Charles Darrow. He became the first board-game millionaire, and a symbol of the quirky unpredictability of the American Dream. The only problem: he didn't invent the game. Some thirty years prior, a woman named Elizabeth Magie created "The Landlord's Game." Its intent was progressive in nature, designed to illustrate the evil of business monopolies. The game was prophetic, coming well in advance of the Great Depression. Ironically, it was this catastrophic era that led to Darrow's unemployment and his subsequent fascination with a game played by some of his Quaker friends in Atlantic City. Darrow would develop this exact variation of the Landlord's Game into his pitch for Parker Brothers, including Atlantic City street names and places. Perversely, Darrow transformed *Monopoly* into a game that seems to celebrate dishonest business practices. On its way to retailing one of the most popular board games in history,

Parker Brothers purchased Magie's patent. The game's original inventor would net a rough total of about $500 for her stroke of gaming genius.

Ada Lovelace: Computer Programming

Lord Byron's daughter, Ada Lovelace, was one of the world's first computer geniuses, though her role is often minimized by male historians. In 1843, the mathematically erudite Lovelace collaborated with inventor Charles Babbage at the University of London. Babbage was working on something called an Analytical Engine, an early prototype of the computer. Lovelace contributed detailed and extensive notes to Babbage's work, particularly by articulating the way Babbage's machine could be fed data to complete complicated math problems, or even compose complex music. These ideas may mark the earliest recorded proposition for what would eventually become computer programming and algorithms. Today, Lovelace's contributions are obscured by debate, and most often by the dismissive and unmistakably misogynistic characterizations of her role.

Margaret Keane: "Big Eyes"

While not technically concerned with an invention, the following is one of the most egregious examples of chauvinistic greed on record. Margaret Keane is an American artist best known for her trademark "Big Eye" paintings, which were popular in the 1960s. The only problem: her fans in the '60s were confident the paintings were done by her husband, Walter. Walter began selling his wife's paintings as his own without permission in the 1950s. Eventually, Margaret discovered what Walter was up to. When she confronted him, Walter used threat, intimidation, and emotional abuse to force her silence. As the works gained in popularity, Margaret continued to toil in obscurity, while Walter enjoyed celebrity. In 1965, the two were divorced. In 1970, Margaret revealed the truth to the public. Walter denied her allegations, which ultimately led to a surreal 1986 courtroom scene in which the two were forced into a head to head paint-off. Walter claimed his sore shoulder prevented him from painting. Naturally, Margaret produced a perfect facsimile of her earlier works, earning the rightful claim to her works in perpetuity.

Trotula of Salerno: Women's Health Findings

Trotula of Salerno is one of the earliest victims of historiographical misogyny. An Italian doctor in the eleventh century who wrote specifically about women's health, she has been recognized as "the world's first gynecologist." Her writings have remained instrumental building blocks in our knowledge about human health, and women's health specifically. And yet, her authorship had been cast into doubt over the ensuing centuries, entirely because historians and medical professionals were skeptical that a woman could have produced works of such accuracy or importance. That's a messed up assumption, but so ingrained was this belief that many even doubted that Trotula of Salerno existed. This convenient doubt ultimately allowed numerous male physicians over subsequent years to cut and paste their own names over her work.

Candace Pert: Neuroscience Findings

While still a graduate student at Johns Hopkins University, Candace Pert discovered the receptor that allows opiates to lock into the brain. This game-changing neuroscience revelation was so important that it led to an award—for her professor. Dr. Solomon Snyder was recognized for his student's achievement. When Pert wrote a letter of protest to the award committee underscoring her determinant contributions, Dr. Snyder mansplained in response, "That's how the game is played."

Of course, men like Dr. Snyder have been playing this game for centuries. But we have an obligation to call them on it. It starts with history. But it continues in modern academia and today's workplace. Let's ensure all the brilliant women in our midst get their due credit. I think we've celebrated more than enough greedy men.

10

Reexamining Women in History Creates a More Nuanced Perspective

Nancy A. Hewitt

Nancy A. Hewitt is a professor of history and women's studies who has taught at Rutgers University, Duke University, and the University of South Florida.

Early women's rights activists tend to be discredited for their lack of support for the abolition movement. One of the issues pushing us to reexamine past historical figures is their attitudes toward past actions that are now deemed immoral, but the past is more nuanced than it looks. Antislavery activists did not necessarily support women's rights, which leads to conflicted emotions toward the movement in the present. Moreover, the women's rights movement consisted of a racially mixed party that viewed vocalizing the sexual abuse of enslaved women as important, facts that are often overlooked in the study of history.

In the years between the 1848 Seneca Falls Woman's Rights Convention and the Civil War, powerful links existed between antislavery and women's rights advocates. Nearly all women's rights advocates supported abolition, but not all abolitionists supported women's rights. Some antislavery activists, of both sexes, thought it was inappropriate for women to be engaged in public and specifically political work. Still, these differences

"Abolition & Suffrage," by Nancy A. Hewitt, author of *Radical Friend: Amy Kirby Post and Her Activist Worlds* (2018), Public Broadcasting Service (PBS). Reprinted by permission.

among abolitionists did not deter the work of those who embraced emancipation for both women and the enslaved.

Those who argued for wider roles for women in the early to mid-nineteenth century called themselves women's (or woman's) rights advocates rather than suffragists. The right to vote was included among their goals, but their agenda was much broader than any single issue. Many of these women were introduced to ideas about sexual and gender equality through the antislavery movement, where the roles of female activists were debated from the 1830s on. The most important debates erupted among members of the American Anti-Slavery Society (AASS), an interracial and mixed-sex organization founded in 1833 under the leadership of William Lloyd Garrison. Members of the AASS insisted that abolition could only be achieved by persuading Americans—slaveholders and non-slaveholders—that human bondage was against God's laws and human morality. The AASS, with its emphasis on moral suasion, provided women and African Americans, many of whom were disenfranchised by state laws in the North, the chance to speak, organize, and write on behalf of the enslaved and to vote, hold office, raise funds, and edit newspapers for the cause. Black and white Garrisonian women used the opportunity to highlight the sexual abuse of enslaved women and girls, which they considered one of the strongest arguments for eradicating slavery.

Lucretia Mott, an avid Garrisonian and a co-founder of the interracial Philadelphia Female Anti-Slavery Society in 1833, was co-organizer of the Seneca Falls Woman's Rights Convention fifteen years later. Like many Garrisonians and many Quakers, she and her husband James refused to participate in electoral politics because they considered the U.S. Constitution a pro-slavery document. Quaker Amy Kirby Post and the famed fugitive Frederick Douglass, who shared Mott's views, were active in the Western New York Anti-Slavery Society, an AASS auxiliary founded in 1841. Six years later, Douglass moved to Rochester to launch his antislavery paper, the *North Star*; and the next summer, he and Post traveled together to Seneca Falls to attend the woman's rights convention.

At Seneca Falls, Douglass supported Elizabeth Cady Stanton's demand for women suffrage while Mott and Post questioned the morality of voting while the federal government was engaged in a war with Mexico that would expand slave territory. Still, the two Quakers believed in principle that women should have the same rights as men and thus signed the Seneca Falls Declaration of Sentiments alongside 98 other women and men. During the 1840s, a growing number of activists argued that the abolition of slavery could only be achieved by wielding political power. They formed the Liberty Party in 1840 and eight years later joined northern Democrats and antislavery Whigs to forge a broader coalition via the Free Soil Party. By then Douglass had embraced this political strategy. Many women, too, supported antislavery political parties, especially in the Midwest. While they served as symbols of morality, fundraisers and organizers of dinners, lectures and other public events, the emphasis on electoral politics ensured that women remained secondary to men in these party organizations.

The outbreak of Civil War brought Garrisonians and Free Soilers together to ensure that the war ended with emancipation and to assist enslaved men, women and children who fled behind Union lines. In the war's aftermath, many abolitionists advocated universal suffrage, that is, the enfranchisement of African Americans and women. However, Republicans in Congress introduced the Fourteenth and Fifteenth Amendments to the U.S. Constitution, extending citizenship and suffrage to black men, including former slaves. The Fourteenth Amendment also introduced the word "male" into the Constitution for the first time. It was in this context, that abolitionists divided over political priorities and suffrage became the defining women's rights issue.

Yet despite the common goal of enfranchisement, women's rights advocates disagreed on tactics and priorities. In November 1869, warring factions established rival organizations. Lucy Stone and Antoinette Brown Blackwell with the support of Stone's husband Henry Blackwell founded the American Woman's Suffrage Association while Susan B. Anthony and Elizabeth Cady Stanton founded the National Woman's Suffrage Association. The American association, which supported the Fifteenth Amendment and accepted male and female members, advocated a state-by-state campaign for women's suffrage. The National association invited only women to participate, opposed the Fifteenth Amendment, and favored a federal amendment as the best means of achieving women's enfranchisement. A third circle of women's rights advocates, including Mott, Post and Sojourner Truth, continued to demand universal suffrage though they more often worked with the National than the American association. Not until 1890, as a younger generation of suffragists took control of the movement, did the rival organizations merge into the National American Woman Suffrage Association. Still, even though the activist coalition of the antebellum era fractured in the late 1860s, the antislavery movement generated critical ideas regarding gender as well as racial equality and served as a crucial training ground for women's rights advocates and suffragists.

11

Reexamining the Past Helps Us Bring Representation to a Wider Audience

Ray Filar

Ray Filar is a freelance political journalist who focuses on women and LGBTQ individuals in politics. Her work has appeared in the Guardian *and the* Times.

In reexamining the past, presentism unearths bits of history that were previously neglected. The United States has only recently allowed same-sex marriage, invigorating an interest in historical LGBTQ figures. But despite the common knowledge that many of the historical figures we celebrate were LGBTQ, not much attention is given to that fact because homosexuality was denigrated in the past. Focusing on these historical figures could help the LGBTQ community find representation in history—and since female representation in general is trailing behind, giving attention to lesbians, bisexual women, and transgender women is even more important.

In these post-*Queer as Folk* times, the word "queer" is rarely said on TV. Not with any approval, anyway. That might be why Channel 4's documentary *Queer as Pop: From Gay Scene to Mainstream*, initially seemed so exciting. If you're part of a subculture whose existence is generally ignored—despite its considerable influence on wider culture—you grasp at any mainstream attempt at representation.

"Where Were All the Lesbians in Queer as Pop?" by Ray Filar, Guardian News and Media Limited, December 30, 2013. Reprinted by permission.

Yet in promising to explore "the men, music and moments that have brought pop music out the closet," this documentary replicated mainstream prejudices by writing women out of its cultural history. Featuring a bland narrative peppered with sweeping generalisations (including the frankly fantastic claim that David Bowie putting his arm around guitarist Mick Ronson on stage was "more important in British pop culture than all the Pride marches, and Stonewall"), the show was livened only by the undeniably great pop music.

The makers of *Queer as Pop* must know that "queer" cannot be reduced to "white gay man." But by the time we got to "if you love dancing, you've probably got a gay man to thank," I found myself checking in the mirror to see if lesbians were still a thing. While they lingered on the formerly male-only London club Heaven and New York's Fire Island with loving nostalgia, women-only clubs like Gateways, open from the 1930s to the 1980s and frequented by bisexual Dusty Springfield, did not receive a single paltry mention. Nor did Springfield herself. The only two female talking heads, Martha Wash, of The Weathergirls, and Angie Bowie, lifted the programme, but there's not much you can do against such a barrage of historical revisionism.

Given the sheer amount of important music lesbian, trans and bisexual women have made during previous decades, our omission from the documentary is no oversight. They even used contemporary queer electroclash artist Peaches' music, without bothering to mention her name. They talked about Sylvester, but what about Joan Armatrading or Tracy Chapman? Why feature Frankie Goes to Hollywood or the Pet Shop Boys while ignoring Wendy Carlos, whose album *Switched-On Bach* and soundtrack to *A Clockwork Orange*, helped to make synths a mainstream instrument?

For that matter, what about riot grrrl, the women-led early-90s movement that paved the way—in prettified and sanitised form— to the Spice Girls? Bands like L7, Sleater-Kinney and Bikini Kill shaped the direction of 90s music, though *Queer as Pop* would apparently prefer to forget about all that. Perhaps the sophisticated links between lesbianism, feminism and gay liberation were a bit complex for a one-hour special pushing the line that the straights loved the queers really.

But what about the myriad women DJs, club promoters and producers who were neither discussed nor asked to discuss themselves? DJ Hannah Holland told me about Smokin Jo: "She was the first and only women to win *DJ Mag* top 100. She was the resident of Trade, London's seminal gay after-hours house night." There wasn't a peep about her. Holland also reminded me of 1930s–40s "undercover lesbian" singer-guitarist Sister Rosetta Tharpe, who was an influence on Elvis Presley and Little Richard. They, of course, were featured while she was not. Speaking of the bravery of early lesbian musical pioneers, I want to know why the show didn't at least briefly mention Alix Dobkin (despite her problematic politics), whose 1973 album *Lavender Jane Loves Women* couldn't really be more overt. And what about Melissa Etheridge, Meshell Ndegeocello, KD Lang, The Raincoats, Skin of Skunk Anansie or Joan Jett?

This kind of revisionism, part of the process by which women are so regularly erased from history, is a common, outdated archiving tactic that gives rise to spurious claims like "women just weren't making good music at the time": an argument which is thrown out blandly about any field of history you might mention, to derail those who know otherwise. This one-dimensional approach to the past gives rise to books like Ernst Gombrich's *The Story of Art*, which did not include not a single woman artist and should more accurately be titled *The Story of Art Made Predominantly by White Western Men*.

People who argue that these histories reflect past merit often naively believe that there will be a tipping point when increasing equality will mean that historical archives reflect social diversity. When future cultural historians look back on today's LGBTQ subcultures, will they credit the sheer amount of exciting, talented women musicians whose work now influences—or is part of—the pop mainstream? I'd like to think that The Gossip, Le Tigre, Angel Haze, The XX, Planningtorock, The Knife, Azealia Banks, Tegan and Sara, and many others, will be given their dues, and that's not even to mention the many artists operating outside of the US/UK imperial hegemony.

Everyone, whatever their sexual orientation, deserves to see portrayals of the past that dig deeper than this. In telling only part of the story, *Queer as Pop* did us a disservice. But with eternal optimism, I'm eagerly anticipating Channel 4's: *Queer as Pop: Everyone We Left Out the First Time*. Who else needs to be in it?

12

The Problem with Dishonoring Christopher Columbus

Gerald Korson

Gerald Korson is a veteran editor and writer in the Catholic press. His work has previously appeared in the Catholic Voice, *the* Catholic Answer, *and* Catholic San Francisco.

The debate over the legacy of Christopher Columbus is a long-standing one, driven primarily by a mistaken understanding of his character and an attack on the Catholic faith. Columbus is still one of the most prominent Catholic figures in history, and he has served as a patron saint to migrating Catholics facing discrimination and violence in the New World. He has undeservedly come to represent all the wrong done in the past when it comes to the genocide of Native Americans, but Columbus was a courageous and pious man who deserves recognition for his accomplishments.

Driven in large part by political correctness and partisan academics and activists, it has become fashionable in recent years to criticize Christopher Columbus and the holiday named in his honor. A closer look, however, reveals the famed explorer to be a man of faith and courage, not a monster.

Many of Columbus' modern critics rely on a warped and politicized reading of history, and it is not the first time the explorer has endured such attacks. When a resurgence of anti-Catholic

"Christopher Columbus and Fake History," by Gerald Korson, Knights of Columbus, September 1, 2017. Reprinted by permission.

bigotry erupted in early 20th-century America, Columbus was a favorite target then as well.

Despite animus among some groups today, the majority of Americans view the explorer positively and with pride. In a K of C-Marist poll from December 2016, 62 percent of Americans expressed a favorable opinion of the explorer and 55 percent said they were in favor of Columbus Day, the holiday named for him. By contrast, fewer than 3 in 10 view Columbus unfavorably and only 37 percent oppose the holiday named for him.

Nonetheless, there have been political efforts to strip Columbus of honor, and the question of whether to continue to recognize Columbus Day is under review in many places. Some states and municipalities have removed the explorer's name from the holiday or eliminated the observance entirely.

A Courageous Journey of Discovery

Unfair attacks on Columbus, past and present, should not be allowed to obscure the truth about the man, his voyage and his motives. Born in Genoa, Italy, Columbus was a deeply Catholic explorer who was willing to go against the grain. He believed he could reach the shores of Asia by sailing a mere 3,000 miles west across the Atlantic. Such a passage would establish faster and easier trade routes than were possible through overland travel or by sailing south and east around Africa.

Scholars of his day calculated the distance to the Orient across the Atlantic at well over 7,000 miles, out of practical range for ships of the day. Those who were skeptical of the admiral's proposal did not hold that the earth was flat, as popular myth has suggested, but rather that it was much larger than Columbus believed. Despite his miscalculation, after 10 weeks Columbus did indeed find land—not the outskirts of the Orient, as he went to his grave believing, but an entirely new continent.

Later, as a nation began to coalesce out of the American colonies, its leaders recognized the admiral's legacy. "Columbia" served as an informal name for what would become the United

States of America. The eventual designation of the nation's capital reflects the esteem the founders had for the Genoese explorer.

Beginning in the 1840s, waves of European immigrants swelled the ranks of Catholics in the United States, and along with that came an increasingly anti-Catholic, anti-immigrant backlash from the Protestant majority. Catholics were subject to discrimination, slander, ridicule, anti-Catholic propaganda and sometimes mob violence.

It was within this hostile climate that Father Michael J. McGivney founded the Knights of Columbus in 1882. He and the founding Knights chose as the Order's patron Christopher Columbus—one of the few Catholics considered a hero of American history. Father McGivney believed the explorer represented both Catholicism and patriotism at the very root of America's heritage, thereby symbolizing that faithful Catholics also can be solid American citizens.

A decade later, as the Order celebrated its patron on the 400th anniversary of his discovery, President Benjamin Harrison proclaimed a national Columbus holiday. He called for "expressions of gratitude to Divine Providence for the devout faith of the discoverer, and for the Divine care and guidance which has directed our history and so abundantly blessed our people."

Colorado became the first state to establish Columbus Day in 1907, and others soon followed. In 1934, with strong urging and support by the Knights, President Franklin D. Roosevelt and Congress made Columbus Day a federal holiday, mandating its first annual observance on Oct. 12, 1937.

Attacks Old and New

As the 1992 quincentenary of Columbus' arrival in the New World approached, vocal opposition to Columbus was heard from partisan and revisionist historians and activists who were often critical of Western civilization as a whole. That year, the city of Berkeley, Calif., changed Columbus Day to Indigenous Peoples

Day, and several other municipalities have made similar moves, often explicitly as a means of dishonoring Columbus.

In response to one such initiative in Baltimore, Eugene F. Rivers III, founder and president of the Seymour Institute for Black Church and Policy Studies, published an op-ed article Dec. 2, 2016.

"To celebrate one cultural group does not require that we denigrate another," he wrote. "Rather than renaming Columbus Day, why not add another holiday, Indigenous Peoples Day, to Baltimore's calendar in honor of Native Americans?"

The 20th century ended with criticism of Columbus and Columbus Day in certain quarters, just as the early 20th century had seen similar opposition.

When the Ku Klux Klan was revived in 1915 and targeted Catholics, Jews and minority groups whom they considered a threat to the nation's "Native, White, Protestant" identity, one of their targets was Columbus.

The Klan opposed the observance of Columbus Day, trying to suppress celebrations of the holiday at the state level. Klan members published articles calling Columbus Day a "papal fraud" and even burned a cross at a Knights of Columbus observance in Pennsylvania.

Today, one can still hear echoes of anti-Catholic prejudice in the modern attacks. For some, Columbus' sponsorship by Spain and introduction of Christianity and Western culture to the lands he discovered make him immediately suspect. The new wave of anti-Columbus attacks go so far as to say that Columbus intended nothing good.

"These criticisms primarily charge Columbus with perpetrating acts of genocide, slavery, 'ecocide,' and oppression," explained Robert Royal, president of the Faith and Reason Institute and author of *1492 and All That: Political Manipulations of History* (1992).

Nonetheless, a closer examination of the record reveals a different picture.

"The dominant picture holds him responsible for everything that went wrong in the New World," wrote Carol Delaney, a former professor at Stanford and Brown universities, in her book *Columbus and the Quest for Jerusalem* (2011). In her opinion, "we must consider his world and how the cultural and religious beliefs of his time colored the way he thought and acted."

In a 2012 *Columbia* interview, Delaney further explained that Columbus found the native peoples to be "very intelligent" and his relations with them "tended to be benign." He gave strict instructions to the settlers to "treat the native people with respect," though some of his men rebelled and disobeyed his orders, particularly during his long absences, Delaney added.

Columbus' voyage made the Old and New Worlds aware of each other for the first time, eventually leading to the founding of new countries in the Western Hemisphere. Diseases inadvertently carried to the New World by the Europeans caused the greatest number of casualties by far, killing some 90 percent of native populations according to some estimates.

"There were terrible diseases that got communicated to the natives," Delaney said, "but he can't be blamed for that."

A Renewed Defense

According to Royal, arguments against Columbus by modern critics often constitute a "new, contemporary form of the 'Black Legend'"—anti-Spanish propaganda dating back to the 16th-century that stereotypes Spanish explorers as uniquely cruel and abusive.

The writings of Bartolomé de las Casas—a 16th-century Spanish Dominican priest, historian and missionary—exposing the abuse of the native peoples are often cited in an effort to impugn Columbus. But while de las Casas lamented the suffering of indigenous people, he also admired and respected Columbus for his "sweetness and benignity" of character, his deep faith and his accomplishments.

"He was the first to open the doors to the ocean sea, where he entered the remote lands and kingdoms which until then had not known our Savior, Jesus Christ, and his blessed name," de las Casas wrote in his *History of the Indies*. While cognizant that Columbus was human and made mistakes, de las Casas never doubted the explorer's good intentions, writing: "Truly, I would not dare blame the admiral's intentions, for I knew him well and I know his intentions are good."

According to Delaney, Columbus "fervently believed it was the duty of every Christian to try to save the souls of non-Christians," and it was this passion that "led him on a great adventure, an encounter such as the world has never seen."

Not surprisingly, popes since the late 19th century have praised Columbus' mission of evangelization. Pope John Paul II, while celebrating Mass at a Columbus monument in the Dominican Republic near the 1992 quincentenary, said the crossshaped memorial "means to symbolize the cross of Christ planted in this land in 1492."

In a speech to the young people of Genoa in May, Pope Francis talked about how a disciple of Christ needs the "virtue of a navigator," and he pointed to the example of Columbus who faced "a great challenge" and showed "courage," a trait he indicated was essential to becoming a "good missionary."

As it did a century ago, the Order is defending Columbus today. When Colorado lawmakers weighed a bill to repeal Columbus Day as a state holiday earlier this year, the Knights of Columbus helped lead the opposition. Recalling the Klan's earlier efforts to oppose Columbus Day, the K of C noted that the measure was not a progressive step but rather "regressive as it takes us back to what the Klan outlined in the 1920s in order to promote ethnic and religious resentment."

The Knights of Columbus has defended its patron from unfair attacks, urging that he continue to receive official recognition as a man of faith and bravery. Columbus represents the kind of heroic courage and religious faith that inspired the establishment of the United States. Although he surely holds special meaning for Catholics and for Italian Americans, Columbus is a figure all citizens of the New World can celebrate.

For this reason, Supreme Knight Carl Anderson said in his annual report this year, "We will continue to defend the truth about Columbus and Columbus Day."

13

Should We Celebrate Christopher Columbus?

Evelyn Red Lodge

Evelyn Red Lodge writes for Writers on the Range *and* Native Sun News Today. *She is a member of the Rosebud Sioux Tribe.*

What we learn in school about how the New World came to be is a slanted narrative. The Americas were not discovered in the manner we tend to learn, as there were already various indigenous nations across the continent. The past reveals a tragedy in which the Native American population significantly dropped with the arrival of European explorers. To this day violence against Native Americans persists. Therefore, by celebrating Christopher Columbus and other past historical figures associated with the subjugation and elimination of Native Americans, we are normalizing what happened and allowing it to continue in the present.

During my 13 years in Rapid City, South Dakota, I've learned that racism and ignorance almost always go hand-in-hand. The West was "won," many people learn in school, but what did westward expansion mean for the Native people who were already living on the land?

The lure of gold brought explorers, miners and then homesteaders to South Dakota during the 19th and early 20th centuries. I imagine that most of those "invaders"—from my point of view—didn't think twice about booting the local people out of the

"Racism Against Native Americans Persists," by Evelyn Red Lodge, High Country News, September 21, 2017.

way. But that was then. The question today is why racism persists when America prides itself on tolerance and respecting diversity.

Here are examples from my life that reveal the kind of blatant racism I've experienced, as well as some of the unconscious racism that is sometimes almost comical.

I go to a Rapid City council meeting where a white local suggests placing statues of Native Americans in Founders Park, rather than in the proposed First Nations Sculpture Gallery in Halley Park. As Native author Elizabeth Cook-Lynn put it, the suggestion was made "without a hint of irony." After all, who were the original founders if not Native people?

I go to the veterans' parade where the 7th United States Cavalry, formed in 1866 to protect homesteaders and raid Native villages, is still honored. These days, of course, more Natives serve in the military per capita than any other ethnic group, according to the director of the National Museum of the American Indian. But few Natives march with the veterans in the parade.

I find a Black Hills trail guide listing the 7th Cavalry Trail as if it's fun for people to follow the trail of mass murderers who killed anywhere from 75 to 125 babies, children and women at Wounded Knee in 1890.

I buy a Happy Meal for my daughter only to find a 7th Cavalry Custer doll inside. She gets upset when I try to explain why I think it belongs in the trash.

In a jewelry shop along Mount Rushmore Road, I look at the gold for which my grandparents' territory was invaded and spot a wine-bottle holder depicting a Native chief chugging a bottle of wine. Old stereotypes die hard. According to a recent study in the journal *Drug and Alcohol Drug Dependence,* alcohol consumption by Natives is shown to be generally less than that of Caucasians in the United States.

Just walking downtown in Rapid City, the so-called City of Presidents, I spot the stores along the way that used to sport signs saying "No Indians or Dogs Allowed." I go to *He Sapa*—the Black Mountains—where I look upon the faces of past US presidents who helped wipe out so many Indigenous peoples. I remember that Natives were only declared to be citizens by the United States Congress less than 100 years ago.

In 2015, I feared to go to any sporting event after a drunk beer salesman poured beer on Native students at a hockey game and shouted, "Go back to the reservation!" Within days, dumping beer on Natives had become a common occurrence at other venues.

I picked up the local newspaper four days after the drunk hockey fan did his business, and the question was raised on the front page: Had the Native students who were attacked stood for the national anthem? (Not that it should make any difference, but it was reported that the students did stand.)

I feared to walk on the north side of Rapid City in 2009 and 2010, after at least two Native families with children were egged while racial slurs were hurled at them. "Go back to where you came from!" is a laughable favorite. One Native woman, who was disabled, was run off the road while driving her car. Urine in bottles was thrown on other Natives. Some Natives were shot with pellet guns.

At the same time—and I am glad to report this—many of the attackers were held accountable after much public outcry:

The jewelry store owner removed the wine holder featuring a drunken Native from her window after local media asked why she'd given it prominence.

The newspaper removed its victim-blaming story from its Internet site.

Two 21-year-old women were arrested in the incident involving the disabled woman, becoming the first in the state to be charged with its new hate-crime law, "malicious intimidation or harassment."

As for failures in the quest for justice, the drunk hockey fan was eventually acquitted of his one and only charge of disorderly conduct. And I am unaware of any charges brought against anyone for the attacks involving egg and urine throwing and pellet guns.

Racism persists, I am sorry to report. I still feel it every day.

14

Patrice Lumumba: Revisiting a Complex Past Event Through a Historical Figure

Georges Nzongola-Ntalaja

Georges Nzongola-Ntalaja is the author of the award-winning book The Congo from Leopold to Kabila: A People's History *and a professor of African studies at the University of North Carolina.*

One of the questions raised by presentism is whether a past action should be labeled as wrong based on present-day attitudes if it was considered right in its time. Furthermore, it is worth examining the polarizing views of certain subject matters and historical figures. Patrice Lumumba is one of the most significant African leaders of the twentieth century, remembered for his fight for an independent Democratic Republic of the Congo. But what does his name mean to people living in Belgium and the United States, nations that plotted his assassination? What aspect of his character and life do we tend to emphasize, and does this cloud our ability to see another side of his story?

Patrice Lumumba, the first legally elected prime minister of the Democratic Republic of the Congo (DRC), was assassinated 50 years ago today, on 17 January, 1961. This heinous crime was a culmination of two inter-related assassination plots by American

"Patrice Lumumba: The Most Important Assassination of the 20th Century," by Georges Nzongola-Ntalaja, Guardian News and Media Limited, January 17, 2011. Reprinted by permission.

and Belgian governments, which used Congolese accomplices and a Belgian execution squad to carry out the deed.

Ludo De Witte, the Belgian author of the best book on this crime, qualifies it as "the most important assassination of the 20th century." The assassination's historical importance lies in a multitude of factors, the most pertinent being the global context in which it took place, its impact on Congolese politics since then and Lumumba's overall legacy as a nationalist leader.

For 126 years, the US and Belgium have played key roles in shaping Congo's destiny. In April 1884, seven months before the Berlin Congress, the US became the first country in the world to recognise the claims of King Leopold II of the Belgians to the territories of the Congo Basin.

When the atrocities related to brutal economic exploitation in Leopold's Congo Free State resulted in millions of fatalities, the US joined other world powers to force Belgium to take over the country as a regular colony. And it was during the colonial period that the US acquired a strategic stake in the enormous natural wealth of the Congo, following its use of the uranium from Congolese mines to manufacture the first atomic weapons, the Hiroshima and Nagasaki bombs.

With the outbreak of the cold war, it was inevitable that the US and its western allies would not be prepared to let Africans have effective control over strategic raw materials, lest these fall in the hands of their enemies in the Soviet camp. It is in this regard that Patrice Lumumba's determination to achieve genuine independence and to have full control over Congo's resources in order to utilise them to improve the living conditions of our people was perceived as a threat to western interests. To fight him, the US and Belgium used all the tools and resources at their disposal, including the United Nations secretariat, under Dag Hammarskjöld and Ralph Bunche, to buy the support of Lumumba's Congolese rivals, and hired killers.

In Congo, Lumumba's assassination is rightly viewed as the country's original sin. Coming less than seven months after independence (on 30 June, 1960), it was a stumbling block to the ideals of national unity, economic independence and pan-African solidarity that Lumumba had championed, as well as a shattering blow to the hopes of millions of Congolese for freedom and material prosperity.

The assassination took place at a time when the country had fallen under four separate governments: the central government in Kinshasa (then Léopoldville); a rival central government by Lumumba's followers in Kisangani (then Stanleyville); and the secessionist regimes in the mineral-rich provinces of Katanga and South Kasai. Since Lumumba's physical elimination had removed what the west saw as the major threat to their interests in the Congo, internationally-led efforts were undertaken to restore the authority of the moderate and pro-western regime in Kinshasa over the entire country. These resulted in ending the Lumumbist regime in Kisangani in August 1961, the secession of South Kasai in September 1962, and the Katanga secession in January 1963.

No sooner did this unification process end than a radical social movement for a "second independence" arose to challenge the neocolonial state and its pro-western leadership. This mass movement of peasants, workers, the urban unemployed, students and lower civil servants found an eager leadership among Lumumba's lieutenants, most of whom had regrouped to establish a National Liberation Council (CNL) in October 1963 in Brazzaville, across the Congo river from Kinshasa. The strengths and weaknesses of this movement may serve as a way of gauging the overall legacy of Patrice Lumumba for Congo and Africa as a whole.

The most positive aspect of this legacy was manifest in the selfless devotion of Pierre Mulele to radical change for purposes of meeting the deepest aspirations of the Congolese people for democracy and social progress. On the other hand, the CNL leadership, which included Christophe Gbenye and Laurent-Désiré Kabila, was more interested in power and its attendant privileges than in the people's welfare. This is Lumumbism in words rather than in deeds. As president three decades later, Laurent Kabila did little to move from words to deeds.

More importantly, the greatest legacy that Lumumba left for Congo is the ideal of national unity. Recently, a Congolese radio station asked me whether the independence of South Sudan should be a matter of concern with respect to national unity in the Congo. I responded that since Patrice Lumumba has died for Congo's unity, our people will remain utterly steadfast in their defence of our national unity.

15

Ronald Reagan's Legacy: Fighting for a United Republican Party

L. John Van Til

Dr. L. John Van Til is the author of Liberty of Conscience: The History of a Puritan Idea *and a retired professor of history and humanities at Grove City College.*

Ronald Reagan served as president of the United States from 1981 to 1989 and made a huge impact on the Republican Party. He is still remembered today for his efforts to bring all conservatives together, whether they were neoconservatives or libertarians. He believed in balancing the government's role in society and giving taxpayers more incentives for their money. He helped rebuild American capitalism, and he was an influential Republican who helped centralize and shape the conservative party for years to come. Looking at his role in building the contemporary Republican Party can give us a better understanding of the party in its present condition.

The passing of Ronald Reagan is a good time to assess his relationship to the Conservative movement in America. Without doubt Reagan shaped its ideology and direction more than any other person in the 20th century, affirming and advancing certain of its ideas while rejecting and ignoring others. A clear understanding of his impact on the face of Conservatism requires a summing up of intellectual currents in the movement

"Ronald Reagan and the Changing Face of Conservatism," by L. John Van Til, The Center for Vision & Values at Grove City College, July 7, 2004. Reprinted by permission.

as he emerged on the national scene. As for defining the term "Conservative," someone once wrote that it is not possible because "too many minds have been trying to 'conserve' too many things for too many reasons for too long."

After years of rummaging around among a myriad of Conservative books, articles, and essays, not to mention hearing dozens of lectures on the subject, it appears to me that the dozens of variations on the term can be boiled down to a few, perhaps four. Many practicing Conservatives will, of course, scream and holler and object vehemently when their particular version is squeezed into one of the divisions proposed here. Even when reduced to a few varieties, however, several themes run through all of them. All, for example, claim to heartily support "freedom" and "liberty," though some do so with only modest enthusiasm (Old Right) while others push freedom to the extreme (Libertarians). It is more obvious that Conservatives all oppose one thing especially—at least in principle—socialism in all its versions, socialism being the idea that government can and should solve all of our problems.

Ronald Reagan made his switch from card-carrying liberal to confirmed Conservative in the years just after World War II. It was at that time that one branch of the Conservative Movement reached its peak and began its rather precipitous decline. Historians refer to this branch as the "Old Right" and agree that its leading spokesman was probably Russell Kirk. Kirk's principal published work, *The Conservative Mind* (1953), appeared early in his career. Like many Old Right Conservatives, Kirk was a Roman Catholic intellectual with a deep affinity for all things old and English, especially for social ideas that flowed from the writings of Edmund Burke. Thus, tradition, customs, civility, manners, morals, and above all, social order were prominent elements in his writings, as in his personal life. It is also fair to say that an anti-modern streak ran through his writings as well. These ideas can be summed up in the proposition that the mere long-time existence of an institution created a presumption that it must have great value.

Implied, therefore, was the idea that old institutions should not be changed except for great cause.

After 15 to 20 years of growth and support by foundations, from the late 1950s to the early 1970s, the Old Right was vigorously challenged by a new breed of Conservative—the Neoconservative. Neoconservatives were converts to the movement from the liberal left. The occasion of their defection and subsequent conversion was what they called a betrayal of the liberal cause by a youthful core of radicals such as Students for a Democratic Society (SDS), radicals who attacked academic standards, encouraged the sexual revolution, and embraced Marxist views. Many Neoconservatives were Jewish intellectuals who were at home in the social sciences and its methods—statistics and computers. Moreover, they were pragmatic and policy-oriented, and this set them apart and in tension with Conservatives of the Old Right who were humanistic scholars—more at home with the ideas of Aristotle than with computers.

The Republican Party, political home of Conservatism, encompassed both the Old Right and Neoconservatives. Both competed for funding from traditionally conservative foundations such as Coors, Scaife, and others, but by the 1980s the Neoconservatives were gaining a larger share of foundation funding. Leaders of the Neoconservative movement included Irving Kristol and Norman Podhoretz, the extended family of each becoming powerful figures in government, journalism, and foundation work. Unlike Old Right Conservatives who wanted to dismantle the welfare state, Neoconservtives assumed the necessity of it but wanted to make it efficient and effective. They also vigorously supported a global democratic order, a view not found among leaders of the Old Right since they were inherently suspicious of democracy, a suspicion they inherited, they said, from the Founding Fathers. When Ronald Reagan came to power in 1981, most of his staff came from the Neoconservative wing of the movement. Old Right attempts to gain seats of power were largely rebuffed, one here and there being given posts such as an Assistant Secretary of Education.

As the Old Right was being marginalized and Neoconservatives were rising to positions of influence and power in the 1970s, a third Conservative faction emerged—the New Right. It is true that it has some ideas in common with the Old Right, such as opposition to communism, support of free markets and limited government, and respect for religion and Judeo-Christian values—the latter honored more in the breach than in practice. Founders of the New Right, including Richard Viguerie, Paul Weyrich, and Phyllis Schlafly, had been active in Republican politics but felt betrayed by its moderate to liberal "Eastern Establishment" leaders. To them, the great majority of Americans endorsed their views, not the views of moderate and liberal Republicans. Though like Old Right leaders in some respects, they came at problems from a business and pragmatic point of view—not from the writings of Aristotle or Edmund Burke. Unhappy with moderate Republicans, and the emerging Neoconservatives, New Right leaders decided to form a new political caucus designed to take over the Republican Party or even to form a new party.

The outstanding feature in the rise of the New Right, however, was the sudden involvement of the Christian Right in the movement. Christians on the Right had been involved in politics for a long time, but now new faces and new issues galvanized a large number of Christian organizations, and they joined hands with the more pragmatic New Right leaders. The Christian Right brought much to the New Right movement—vast television and radio audiences, millions more listening in the pews, a moral fervor, and a deep patriotic appeal. Its leading figures were Pat Robertson and Jerry Falwell. One issue more than any other brought the Christian Right out of the churches and into the political fray—the *Roe* abortion decision of 1973. It was not long before other social issues were tied to it, including prayer in public schools, Supreme Court appointments, and the like.

The Christian element of the New Right suffered the same destiny as the Old Right at the hands of the Reagan administration. Their ideas were honored with lip service but not with policy initiatives supported vigorously by the President. The Christian Right continued, however, to vote Republican by the millions—even voting for Bush, the Elder.

In addition to the Old Right, Neoconservatives, and the New Right, a fourth group claimed citizenship in the kingdom of Conservatism in the post–World War II era—they styled themselves "Libertarians." Libertarians have always argued vigorously about who they are and which of them truly represents the essence of their movement. They do so because the core idea that drives them all is the notion that each person is autonomous. Not all of them state their premise quite that starkly, but personal autonomy is nevertheless the central idea for them. From a distance, it is clear that Libertarians have their roots largely in the works of two intellectuals—the Austrian economist Mises and the anarco-capitalist Murray Rothbard. Most Libertarians focus on economic issues and the need to be free from all government contact and control. One admiring biographer of Rothbard captured this mood when he entitled his book about him *An Enemy of the State*. As for moral principles in typical Libertarian thinking, a paraphrase of a line from the Book of Genesis will do: "Each man did what was right in his own eyes," and they would add "as long as it does not injure anyone else." Contemporary expressions of a Libertarian outlook may be found in the Reason Foundation and Cato Institute—a look at their websites will make this clear.

All four of these branches of Conservatism were hard at work as Ronald Reagan matured as a Conservative and then achieved political power. Great reader that he was, it may be assumed that Reagan was familiar with most ideas emanating from these groups. The question remains, however, as to how Reagan related to them. In answering that question we can see how Reagan changed the face of Conservatism. This could be the subject of a whole book, but here it will be briefly sketched.

Reagan was famous for his statement, paraphrased here, "Thou shalt not speak evil of fellow Republicans," and that would, of course, also refer to Conservatives. In a word, he appreciated the efforts of all Conservatives and said so. Significantly, however, he used only those ideas that fit with his well-developed public philosophy and his sense of mission. Rebuilding the American economy was one of two central pillars of his mission as a politician. The other was the defeat, not the containment of, Communism. He gathered ideas and policy suggestions from all quarters of Conservatism that might help him achieve his mission. As it turned out, many ideas of the Neoconservative branch of the movement fit well with his goals, more so than ideas from the other branches.

Being a born-again Christian, especially evident from recent books about his faith, Reagan was very sensitive to numerous social issues that were near and dear to the hearts of the Christian element of the New Right. He spoke to that constituency often about these ideas, including abortion and pornography. When it came to legislation about these matters, however, he did little—sensing, no doubt, that they were more divisive than constructive in the public square. Stated another way, he was not willing to see these issues undermine the two main goals of his mission. As one writer put it, in the end these issues "were window dressing" in the larger plan of his administration.

Reagan's plan to rebuild American capitalism, a capitalism which had faltered for 20 years under the influence of John K. Galbraith's doctrine of an "affluent society," assumed limits for government—something less than the New Deal and Great Society had put in place. This is not what the Old Right, the New Right, and Libertarians heard. They thought he meant to roll back government and radically shrink it to a size they imagined, eliminating huge programs such as Social Security along the way. Reagan did not think in these terms, rather, he thought more of efficiency—more bang for the taxpayer's buck. Stated another way, Reagan wanted to make government work better, not merely make it smaller. Further, he wanted government to be less intrusive in the daily lives of citizens as they sought to make their way in life. Neoconservatives were more attuned to this view and were, thus, the main beneficiaries of Reagan's economic stance. Their manta was "democratic capitalism," not free market economics. In short, Neoconservatives ended up being appointed to many important posts of Reagan's government.

And, the Neoconservatives were also well-positioned to advise Reagan on foreign policy. Generally, they favored communism's extinction rather than its containment. Further, as proponents of "democratic capitalism" they were for expanding world trade— rather than being supporters, as others of their Conservative brethren were, of a cranky economic isolationism.

Ronald Reagan was in the right place at the right time to pull together a coalition of Conservatives—various Republicans, and socially and economically conservative Democrats—to form a powerful alliance. As recent Reagan memorial services indicated, this alliance empowered him to achieve great things, including his twin goals—the defeat of communism and the revival of the American economy. A decade's distance from his successes in these matters makes it clear that Reagan the man had pulled together a coalition of Conservative factions, and others, to achieve his goals. It is also clear that social and moral reform was not part of his program though some Conservatives were hopeful that it was at the time.

Reagan did change the face of Conservatism through the sheer power of his personality and ability to engineer the political process. From the distance of 15 years it is clear that ideas he supported gained prominence in the Conservative movement while those ideas he ignored tended to fall by the way. For example, Neoconservative ideas about economics and governmental power continue to be prominently reflected in the Republican Party. That is, it still supports government on a scale similar to the Democrats and it assumes that government should tinker with the markets as opposed to being completely free as other branches of Conservatism teach. Obviously, ideas of the Old

Right and Libertarians—fully free markets and no or very limited government—have fallen upon deaf ears in government circles. A glance at the Bush administration today confirms this pattern.

And what about the Old Right and Libertarians as players in the larger Conservative movement? The Old Right hangs on in the academy, at conferences, and in journals few people read. As for Libertarians, many of them have morphed into new forms, hoping to have some influence on public policy, a point evident in the programs and literature of the Cato Institute and the Reason Foundation. Harsher elements of the Libertarian view—personal moral autonomy for example—have been softened into more palatable forms for consumption among traditional Conservatives. As for the New Right with its strong Christian Right influence, it hangs on too and hopes that Bush, the Younger will lead America into the promised land of higher moral standards.

The 2004 elections will tell us much about the health of Conservatism. Will it survive? The 2000 election suggested that Conservative power was waning if not on the ropes. Ironically, it has evolved in the past to meet changing conditions as it did in the hands of Ronald Reagan. Still, Conservatism may end up on the fringes of American politics, in the wilderness as it were, until another Ronald Reagan arrives to lead. It seems clear that if another Conservative (Republican) wished to lead in the Reagan mold he would need very clearly articulated goals and a very forceful, winsome personality.

16

Why Ronald Reagan's Legacy Should Be Revisited

Jeralyn Merritt

Jeralyn Merritt is a television legal analyst and a criminal defense lawyer based in Denver. She is also the founder of the blog Talkleft: The Politics of Crime.

In light of the opioid crisis, the crack epidemic of the 1980s and 1990s is being revisited along with President Ronald Reagan's attitude toward it and how it was handled by his administration. Reagan's legacy is a contentious one. He is remembered for his influence on the Republican Party, but he is also remembered for his involvement in the drug epidemic affecting black communities, his failure to respond to the AIDS crisis that affected mostly gay men, and his policies on women's reproductive rights.

A s Reagan's deification by the media and the right reaches epic proportions, three of his less-than-endearing legacies deserve to be highlighted:

- Mandatory minimum drug sentences in 1986. This was the first time Congress passed mandatory minimum sentences since the Boggs Act in 1951.
- Federal sentencing guidelines: Under this new method of sentencing, which went into effect in 1987, prison time is determined mostly by the weight of the drugs involved in

"Reagan's Drug War Legacy," by Jeralyn Merritt, Alternet/Alternet.org, June 18, 2004. Reprinted by permission.

the offense. Parole was abolished and prisoners must serve 85 percent of their sentence. Except in rare situations, judges can no longer factor in the character of the defendant, the effect of incarceration on his or her dependents, and in large part, the nature and circumstances of the crime. The only way to receive a more lenient sentence is to act as an informant against others and hope that the prosecutor is willing to deal. The guidelines in effect stripped Article III of their sentencing discretion and turned it over to prosecutors.

- The Anti-Drug Abuse Act of 1988: This law established a federal death penalty for "drug kingpins." President Reagan called it a new sword and shield in the escalating battle against drugs, and signed the bill in his wife's honor:

Nancy, for your tireless efforts on behalf of all of us, and the love you've shown the children in your Just Say No program, I thank you and personally dedicate this bill to you. And with great pleasure, I will now sign the Anti-Drug ...

Did the law nab Pablo Escobar? No. The law's first conquest was David Ronald Chandler, known as "Ronnie." Ronnie grew marijuana in a small town in rural, northeast Alabama. About 300 pounds a year. Ronnie was sentenced to death for supposedly hiring someone to kill his brother-in-law. The witness against him later recanted. Clinton commuted Chandler's death sentence to life.

While we agree Nancy Reagan is to be lauded for her caretaking of her husband the past ten years, we must also point out that she is responsible for the "Just Say No" campaign against drugs, which ultimately deteriorated into a punchline. Remember this famous Nancy quote?

Not long ago in Oakland, Calif., I was asked by a group of children what to do if they were offered drugs. And I answered, "Just Say No." Soon after that those children in Oakland formed a Just Say No Club and now there are over 10,000 such clubs all over the country.

As a result of these flawed drug policies initiated by then President Reagan, (and continued by Bush I, Clinton and Bush

II) the number of those imprisoned in America has quadrupled to over 2 million. These are legacies that groups like Families Against Mandatory Minimums are still fighting today. Even George Shultz, Ronald Reagan's former secretary of state, acknowledged in 2001 that the War on Drugs is a flop.

In *Smoke and Mirrors*, Dan Baum, a former *Wall Street Journal* reporter, provides a detailed account of the politics surrounding Reagan's war on drugs.

> *Conservative parents' groups opposed to marijuana had helped to ignite the Reagan Revolution. Marijuana symbolized the weakness and permissiveness of a liberal society; it was held responsible for the slovenly appearance of teenagers and their lack of motivation. Carlton Turner, Reagan's first drug czar, believed that marijuana use was inextricably linked to "the present young-adult generation's involvement in anti-military, anti-nuclear power, anti-big business, anti-authority demonstrations." A public-health approach to drug control was replaced by an emphasis on law enforcement. Drug abuse was no longer considered a form of illness; all drug use was deemed immoral, and punishing drug offenders was thought to be more important than getting them off drugs. The drug war soon became a bipartisan effort, supported by liberals and conservatives alike. Nothing was to be gained politically by defending drug abusers from excessive punishment.*
>
> *Drug-control legislation was proposed, almost like clockwork, during every congressional-election year in the 1980s. Election years have continued to inspire bold new drug-control schemes. On September 25 of last year Speaker of the House Newt Gingrich introduced legislation demanding either a life sentence or the death penalty for anyone caught bringing more than two ounces of marijuana into the United States. Gingrich's bill attracted twenty-six co-sponsors, though it failed to reach the House floor. A few months earlier Senator Phil Gramm had proposed denying federal welfare benefits, including food stamps, to anyone convicted of a drug crime, even a misdemeanor. Gramm's proposal was endorsed by a wide variety of senators—including liberals such as Barbara Boxer, Tom Harkin, Patrick Leahy, and Paul Wellstone. A revised version of the amendment, limiting the punishment to people*

convicted of a drug felony, was incorporated into the welfare bill signed by President Clinton during the presidential campaign. Possessing a few ounces of marijuana is a felony in most states, as is growing a single marijuana plant. As a result, Americans convicted of a marijuana felony, even if they are disabled, may no longer receive federal welfare or food stamps. Convicted murderers, rapists, and child molesters, however, will continue to receive these benefits.

Reagan also left his mark on the Supreme Court. He nominated conservative Justices Antonin Scalia, Anthony Kennedy and Sandra Day O'Connor to sit on the Court and appointed William Rehnquist as Chief Justice. The Supreme Court has upheld these draconian laws and sentencing guidelines, as well as the 1984 Federal Bail Reform Act, which allows prosecutors to request that drug defendants facing a possible sentence of ten years or more be held without bond until trial.

Organizations to Contact

The editors have compiled the following list of organizations concerned with the issues debated in this book. The descriptions are derived from materials provided by the organizations. All have publications or information available for interested readers. The list was compiled on the date of publication of the present volume; the information provided here may change. Be aware that many organizations take several weeks or longer to respond to inquiries, so allow as much time as possible.

African American Intellectual History Society (AAIHS)
History Department, Garinger 110
9201 University City Blvd.
Charlotte, NC 28223
email: aaihs10@gmail.com
website: https://www.aaihs.org

The AAIHS is a member-based organization focusing on black culture and ideas. Its main purpose is to help promote African American history as a growing field of study. Through *Black Perspectives*, a blog maintained by AAIHS contributors, readers will find cutting-edge posts and essays on past historical figures like Langston Hughes.

Association for the Study of African American Life and History (ASALH)
Howard Center
2225 Georgia Ave. NW, Suite 331
Washington, DC 20059
phone: (202) 238-5910
email: asalh.org/contact-us/
website: https://asalh.org

The ASALH was founded in 1915 by Dr. Carter G. Woodson. This organization initiated Black History Month, and its goal is to spread information about the history and culture of people of African descent to a global community. Among its activities, it hosts an annual convention and essay contests for undergraduate and graduate students.

Association of Black Women Historians (ABWH)
PO Box 35767
Los Angeles, CA 90035-0767
email: info@abwh.org
website: http://truth.abwh.org

Three African American historians—Rosalyn Terborg-Penn, Eleanor Smith, and Elizabeth Parker—started the ABWH when they saw the need to create a support network for black women in the history field. The mission of this organization is not only promoting the work of black women historians and helping them find opportunities but fostering research on black history as well. One of the achievements of this organization is its involvement in fostering black history in postsecondary education.

Charles H. Wright Museum of African American History
315 E. Warren Ave.
Detroit, MI 48201
phone: (313) 494-5800
email: info@thewright.org
website: http://thewright.org

This museum, based in Detroit, Michigan, was founded in 1965. Its core mission is to educate a wider audience on the history and culture of African Americans. Its archive contains over thirty-five thousand documents and artifacts, and it served as the first African American museum in Detroit.

Conference on Latin American History
Department of History
University of North Carolina at Charlotte
9201 University City Blvd.
Charlotte, NC 28223
phone: (704) 687-5129
email: clah-uncc@uncc.edu
website: http://clah.h-net.org

The Conference on Latin American History, which is affiliated with the American Historical Association, works on disseminating information about Latin America. Its goal is to advance the study of Latin American history and to improve the way it is taught. The conference is an independent initiative, and all interested in the history of this region are welcome to become members.

The Mariners' Museum and Park (The Ages of Exploration)
100 Museum Dr.
Newport News, VA 23606
phone: (757) 596-2222
email: frontdeskstaff@MarinersMuseum.org
website: http://exploration.marinersmuseum.org

Established in 1930, the Mariners' Museum and Park is home to more than 1 million maritime materials. Its collection makes it one of the largest maritime museums in the world. The exploration section of its website offers information about different explorers from the past, including Christopher Columbus.

Middle Atlantic Council of Latin American Studies (MACLAS)
c/o Bridget Chesterton
Associate Professor of History & Social Studies Education
State University of New York Buffalo State
Buffalo, NY 14222
phone: (716) 878-4323
email: chestebm@buffalostate.edu
website: http://www.maclas.org

The MACLAS hosts an annual conference to bring together scholars in the mid-Atlantic region (Delaware, the District of Columbia, Maryland, New Jersey, New York, Pennsylvania, Virginia, and West Virginia). The goal of this association is to share research on the Latin American region. In 2017, the committee launched a peer-reviewed journal on Latin America titled *Middle Atlantic Review of Latin American Studies*.

National History Day (NHD)
4511 Knox Rd., Suite 205
College Park, MD 20740
phone: (301) 314-9739
email: info@nhd.org
website: https://www.nhd.org

The goal of the NHD is to actively engage students in learning about history. It offers hands-on opportunities through contests and also helps teachers find creative ways to make learning about history a more fascinating process.

National Museum of the American Indian (NMAI)
Fourth St. SW & Independence Ave. SW
Washington, DC 20560
phone: (202) 633-1000
email: nmai-info@si.edu
website: http://nmai.si.edu

The NMAI is a branch of the Smithsonian Institution. This museum preserves one of the largest collections of indigenous artifacts, documents, and archival materials in the world. It includes three centers based in Washington, DC; New York City; and Suitland, Maryland. Additionally, the NMAI focuses on community programs and traveling exhibitions to further its mission.

Native Americans and Indigenous Studies Association
c/o Noelani Goodyear-Kaʻōpua (Kanaka Maoli)
Associate Professor
Department of Political Science
University of Hawaiʻi at Mānoa
2424 Maile Way, Saunders 640
Honolulu, HI 96822
email: contact.naisa@gmail.com
website: https://www.naisa.org

The Native Americans and Indigenous Studies Association is the largest organization focused on indigenous studies. It is a member-based, international organization that started in 2007. It maintains the *Native American and Indigenous Studies* journal published by University of Minnesota Press.

Omohundro Institute of Early American History & Culture
PO Box 8781
Williamsburg, VA 23187-8781
phone: (757) 221-1114
email: oieahc@wm.edu
website: https://oieahc.wm.edu

The goal of this organization, founded in 1943, is to support research on early American history. To do so, it offers various fellowship opportunities, publishes the leading journal on early American history, the *William and Mary Quarterly*, and hosts events to promote networking among scholars in the field.

Organization of American Historians (OAH)

112 N. Bryan Ave.
Bloomington, IN 47408-4141
phone: (812) 855-7311
email: oah@oah.org
website: http://www.oah.org

The OAH is described as the largest professional association for the study of American history. It was established in 1907, and its mission consists of three principles: the advancement of scholarship, historical advocacy, and professional integrity. Its membership includes university professors, archivists, museum curators, and students.

Society for Historians of American Foreign Relations (SHAFR)

SHAFR Business Office
Department of History
Middle Tennessee State University
1301 E. Main St., Box 23
Murfreesboro, TN 37132
phone: (617) 458-6156
email: amy.sayward@shafr.org
website: http://www.shafr.org

The SHAFR was founded in 1967 to help create a common ground for scholars and students focusing on the history of American foreign relations. It holds an annual meeting and publishes a journal, *Diplomatic History*, which covers the United States' international history and foreign relations, along with grand strategy, diplomacy, and issues on gender, race, and ideology.

Bibliography

Books

Joyce Appleby, Lynn Hunt, and Margaret Jacob, *Telling the Truth About History*. New York, NY: W. W. Norton & Company, 1994.

Craig Bourne, *A Future for Presentism*. Oxford, UK: Clarendon Press, 2006.

Hal Brands and Jeremi Suri, eds., *The Power of the Past: History and Statecraft*. Washington, DC: Brookings Institution Press, 2016.

Dinesh D'Souza, *Ronald Reagan: How an Ordinary Man Became an Extraordinary Leader*. New York, NY: Touchstone, 1997.

David Hackett Fischer, *Historians' Fallacies: Toward a Logic of Historical Thought*. New York, NY: First Harper Torchbook, 1970.

Evelyn Gajowski, ed., *Presentism, Gender, and Sexuality in Shakespeare*. Basingstoke, UK: Palgrave MacMillan, 2009.

Sam Harris, *The Moral Landscape: How Science Can Determine Human Values*. New York, NY: Free Press, 2010.

François Hartog, *Regimes of Historicity: Presentism and Experiences of Time*. New York, NY: Columbia University Press, 2003.

Carol Hymowitz and Michaele Weissman, *A History of Women in America: From Founding Mothers to Feminists—How Women Shaped the Life and Culture of America*. New York, NY: Bantam Books, 1978.

Alexander Kennedy, *Columbus: Lies of a New World*. Seattle, WA: Amazon Digital Services LLC, 2016.

Barbara MacKinnon and Andrew Fiala, *Ethics: Theory and Contemporary Issues*. Boston: MA: Wadsworth Publishing, 2014.

Ernâni Magalhães and Nathan L. Oaklander, eds., *Presentism: Essential Readings*. Washington, DC: Lexington Books, 2010.

Janice North, Karl C. Alvestad, and Elena Woodacre, eds., *Premodern Rulers and Postmodern Viewers: Gender, Sex, and Power in Popular Culture*. Basingstoke, UK: Palgrave MacMillan, 2018.

Russ Shafer-Landau, *The Fundamentals of Ethics*. Oxford, UK: Oxford University Press, 2017.

Margot Lee Shetterly, *Hidden Figures: The American Dream and the Untold Story of the Black Women Mathematicians Who Helped Win the Space Race*. New York, NY: William Morrow, 2016.

Jakob Wassermann, *Columbus, Don Quixote of the Seas*. New York, NY: Little, Brown, and Company, 1930.

Leo Zeilig, *Lumumba: Africa's Lost Leader*. London, UK: Haus Publishing, 2008.

Periodicals and Internet Sources

Associated Press, "Tennessee Lawmakers Punish Memphis for Removing Confederate Statues," NBC News, April 18, 2018. https://www.nbcnews.com/news/us-news/tennessee -lawmakers-punish-memphis-removing-confederate -statues-n866961.

Paul Bartow, "The Growing Threat of Historical Presentism," *AEIdeas* (blog), AEI, December 10, 2015. http://www .aei.org/publication/the-growing-threat-of-historical -presentism/.

Lou Cannon, "Ronald Reagan: Impact and Legacy," Miller Center, n.d. https://millercenter.org/president/reagan/impact-and-legacy.

CBC Radio, "The Allure and the Dangers of 'Presentism,'" March 18, 2016. http://www.cbc.ca/radio/thesundayedition/the-past-is-not-the-present-do-food-animals-have-rights-alberto-manguel-s-curious-mind-the-great-hunger-1.3497315/the-allure-and-the-dangers-of-presentism-1.3497463.

Ta-Nehisi Coates, "The Legacy of Malcolm X," *Atlantic*, May 2011. https://www.theatlantic.com/magazine/archive/2011/05/the-legacy-of-malcolm-x/308438/.

David Davenport, "Presentism: The Dangerous Virus Spreading Across College Campuses," *Forbes*, December 1, 2015. https://www.forbes.com/sites/daviddavenport/2015/12/01/presentism-the-dangerous-virus-spreading-across-college-campuses/#6fb059ff2dcb.

Peter Dreier, "Reagan's Real Legacy," *Nation*, February 4, 2011. https://www.thenation.com/article/reagans-real-legacy/.

Brynn Holland, "11 of History's Fiercest Females Everyone Should Know," History.com, March 7, 2017. https://www.history.com/news/11-of-historys-fiercest-females-everyone-should-know.

Jaweed Kaleem, "First It Was Confederate Monuments. Now Statues Offensive to Native Americans Are Poised to Topple Across the U.S.," *Los Angeles Times*, April 1, 2018. http://www.latimes.com/nation/la-na-native-american-statue-removal-20180401-story.html.

Antoine Roger Lokongo, "Patrice Lumumba's Relevance," *Pambazuka News*, January 16, 2013. https://www.pambazuka.org/governance/patrice-lumumba%E2%80%99s-relevance.

Madison Park, "San Francisco to Remove What's Been Called a 'Racist and Disrespectful' Statue," CNN, March 8, 2018. https://www.cnn.com/2018/03/08/us/san-francisco-statue -native-american-man-trnd/index.html.

Michael Signer, "I'm a Progressive Mayor. Here's Why I Voted No on Removing My City's Confederate Statue," *Washington Post*, May 24, 2017. https://www.washingtonpost.com /posteverything/wp/2017/05/24/im-a-progressive-mayor -heres-why-i-voted-no-on-removing-my-citys-confederate -statue/?noredirect=on&utm_term=.896d615986f9.

Stanford Encyclopedia of Philosophy, "Presentism," January 22, 2018. https://plato.stanford.edu/entries/presentism /#MotiPres.

Burton Yale, "The Ten Legacies of Ronald Reagan," Heritage Foundation, November 15, 1988. https://www.heritage.org /political-process/report/the-ten-legacies-ronald-reagan.

Howard Zinn, "The Real Christopher Columbus," *Jacobin*, October 12, 2015. https://www.jacobinmag.com/2014/10 /the-real-christopher-columbus/.

Index